A Scholarly Edition of a Seventeenth-Century Anonymous Commonplace Book in the British Library

How People Received and Responded to the Books They Read

A Scholarly Edition of a Seventeenth-Century Anonymous Commonplace Book in the British Library

How People Received and Responded to the Books They Read

Catherine Armstrong

With a Foreword by
Maureen Bell

The Edwin Mellen Press
Lewiston•Lampeter

Library of Congress Cataloging-in-Publication Data

Library of Congress Control Number: 2014930590

Armstrong, Catherine Mary.
   A scholarly edition of a seventeenth-century anonymous commonplace book in the British library : how people received and responded to the books they read / Catherine Mary Armstrong ; with a foreword by Maureen Bell.
1. Literary criticism--European--English. 2. Literary criticism--Books and reading. 3. Literary criticism--Semiotics and theory.
      p. cm.
   Includes bibliographical references..
   ISBN-13: 978-0-7734-0084-9 (hardcover)
   ISBN-10: 0-7734-0084-2 (hardcover)
   I. Title.

hors série.

A CIP catalog record for this book is available from the British Library.

Copyright © 2014 Catherine Armstrong

All rights reserved. For information contact

      The Edwin Mellen Press   The Edwin Mellen Press, Ltd.
      Box 450   Lampeter
      Lewiston, New York   Ceredigion, Wales
      USA 14092-0450   United Kingdom SA48 8LT

Printed in the United States of America

Dedication

This book is dedicated to my parents, Maureen and Michael Armstrong, whose interest in my work always inspires me, and to my husband, Michael Batchelor, without whom this book would never have been finished.

Table of Contents

Abstract	i
Foreword	iii
Introduction	1
Editorial Note	14
Bibliography of books on commonplacing	16
List of paragraphs	18
Modern Edition	21
Bibliography of books used by author	177

Abstract

This is a scholarly edition of a manuscript commonplace book found in the Harleian collection of the British Library. It consists of thirty-three folio pages of notes broken down into sixty-one numbered paragraphs in the same hand describing information retrieved from a number of different books. This annotated edition of shows what and how this person read. Based on clues within the text the commonplace book was probably written around 1670. The identity of the author remains a mystery although tantalising clues appear within the text and I tentatively suggest that the author is George Bohun. The reader does not make direct reference to any of his sources but the similarity of the manuscript text to the printed texts makes their association very clear. An example of a book used by the commonplacer to make these notes is Samuel Purchas's 1625 multi-volume work *Purchas His Pilgrimage*.

Foreword

'Unlike modern readers, who follow the flow of a narrative from beginning to end, early modern Englishmen read in fits and starts and jumped from book to book. They broke texts into fragments and assembled them into new patterns by transcribing them in different sections of their notebooks. Then they reread the copies and rearranged the patterns while adding more excerpts. Reading and writing were therefore inseparable activities. They belonged to a continuous effort to make sense of things, for the world was full of signs: you could read your way through it; and by keeping an account of your readings, you made a book of your own, one stamped with your personality. . . .'

Robert Darnton, "Extraordinary Commonplaces," *The New York Review of Books*, December 21, 2000

The field of study known broadly as 'the history of the book' is a capacious one, taking in every aspect of textual production, circulation and reception. In recent years the focus amongst early modern scholars of book history has shifted somewhat, away from the enumeration of texts or research into the economics of book production and towards the elusive activities of readers. Exactly which printed books and manuscripts were read, by whom and in what circumstances, are questions now pursued by cultural, social and political historians as well as by bibliographers and literary researchers. Drawing on Renaissance theories of reading as well as more recent theories of reader-reception, scholars are interrogating afresh the material traces of past reading practices. Discovering *how*, as well as *what*, people read is central to book history's current research focus. Lisa Jardine and Anthony Grafton's study of Gabriel Harvey's reading, Kevin Sharpe's investigation of Sir William Drake's reading notes, and Heidi Brayman Hackel's work on reading and gender, with its reconstruction of the Countess of Bridgewater's library, are prominent in leading the way as exemplary studies of this kind.

Not surprisingly, the early modern readers who have left the most obvious evidence of their reading were those wealthy enough to amass considerable personal libraries. Some book collections are still physically accessible in great houses or as part of larger institutional libraries, while others now dispersed are at least capable of reconstruction through ownership marks, or through surviving catalogues and inventories. But the books bought or otherwise acquired do not provide unequivocal evidence about which of them was actually read by its owner. Still less can they tell us *how* they were read, absorbed and used. Books which carry the owner's handwritten additions – marginal annotations, amendments, exclamations and sometimes extensive notes – can certainly bring us nearer to the reader's engagement with what was read; and diaries and letters sometimes offer significant complementary information about motivations and reactions.

Amongst these, often fragmentary, traces of readers and their reading practices, the commonplace book has a special significance. Commonplacing was a skill learnt in youth, and sometimes maintained throughout adulthood, as a way of recording and organizing notes, gathered while reading, of striking or potentially useful facts, arguments, information and ideas. They were practical notebooks, compiled sometimes over long periods of time and designed to be augmented, re-read and revisited in the future. As both a record of topics read or researched and a repository of passages and references, the commonplace book can provide a glimpse of the historical reader's interests and direct engagement with a range of reading matter. Identifying exactly what was selected for copying into a commonplace book, as well as the extent to which the chosen extracts were ordered and altered by the copyist, can bring us as close to the act of reading, and to the mentalités of historically distant readers, as we are likely to be able to reach.

Until recently, the commonplace books of the period which have attracted scholarly attention and which have appeared in modern editions have been those of prominent writers and thinkers such as Francis Bacon, Ben Jonson, John Milton, and John Locke. Now, however, the field is widening as the notebooks of less exalted figures are discovered and studied. Inevitably, since they were predominantly written by professional men (though, occasionally, by godly gentlewomen), commonplace books often consist principally of Biblical extracts, or authorities on the law, or extracts from classical writers. Catherine

Armstrong's edition of this anonymous seventeenth-century example is of particular interest, since it is testimony to a different kind of reader whose interests were rather different from the usual pattern. In making it accessible, she provides a welcome new addition to our range of evidence for the experience of reading. Found amongst the Harleian Manuscripts at the British Library, this commonplace book is anonymous and undated and gives no information about its sources. Dr Armstrong has not only identified the sources used and compared them carefully with the manuscript, but has also deduced the commonplace book's date of composition as being between the late 1670s and early 1680s. She is able, moreover, to suggest as a possible author George Bohun, a translator and merchant who became MP for Coventry. Bohun's interests certainly chime with some of the preoccupations evident in the compilation, and Dr Armstrong assesses the evidence judiciously and cautiously to make a persuasive case for Bohun's possible authorship.

By contrast with the more familiar literary or professional commonplacer, the author of this particular compilation exhibits a range of interests without following any obvious system of organization. . The extracts here are not ordered methodically by topic or by heading, but seem to follow the reader's interest of the moment, sometimes interrupting one subject with material on another. Fascinated by travel and geography, the compiler read tales of exploration and was drawn especially to information about the fauna of the New World. He read and recorded stories from history, and delighted in unusual events such as the explosion of William the Conqueror's corpse and the beheading of Mary, Queen of Scots. He was fascinated by monarchs and aristocracy, by ritual and hierarchy, and was alive to the turns of fortune attending those in power. The twists and turns of the continental as well as English Reformation were also of particular concern. In tracking down his sources, and detailing the changes, amendments and additions introduced by the copyist, Dr Armstrong brings into focus a reader of sometimes contradictory sympathies, or at least wide and occasionally apparently incongruous reading habits. Extracts from anti-Catholic works, for example, appear alongside others with a more sympathetic view. Such inconsistencies, however, arguably bring into focus a more convincingly complex, lively and enquiring reader than would a more programmatically coherent manuscript. Most importantly, Dr Armstrong's edition enables us – through her identification of sources, alterations, minor adjustments and juxtapositions – to catch sight of an individual seventeenth-century reader making sense of the world through his engagement with books.

Maureen Bell

University of Birmingham

Acknowledgements

I would like to thank Professor Bernard Capp (University of Warwick), Dr. Maureen Bell (University of Birmingham) and Dr. John Hinks (University of Leicester) for their helpful and insightful remarks and friendly support, which allowed me to bring this project to fruition.

Introduction

The study of commonplace books offers an important means for scholars to gather evidence on the history of reading practices in early modern England. A cross between a diary and a notebook, a commonplace book is usually a collection of handwritten notes in which a reader recorded items of particular interest from printed books, manuscripts or from conversations or sermons. Some commonplace books are interspersed with notes, messages, shopping lists, even illustrations, while others are extremely orderly reflections of serious scholarship, some being divided up thematically with indexes. A formal Renaissance commonplace book acted as a repository of pithy sayings that could be used to enhance one's own conversation and writing. However, it is important not to adopt too narrow a definition of a commonplace book because it has much in common with other engagements with print culture such as scrapbooking. Classical and biblical references commonly appear, reflecting the education and typical reading habits of the time. Commonplacing is sometimes considered a substitute for writing notes in the margins of a book's printed text, which might indicate that the commonplace author had only limited access to the volume i.e. that he did not own it. We can thus use commonplace books to learn something about book ownership and the circumstances in which the books were read because commonplacing was also a reflection of the particular market for books in the early modern period. Books (especially large multi-volume works) were very expensive and even a wealthy member of the elite might not possess a large library. Books were often borrowed from acquaintances or used at their homes. Many town libraries were founded during this period and a few lucky readers living nearby had access to their books. To gather information, a reader may have had only a few hours to copy as much as possible before then returning the book to its owner or passing it on to another borrower.

Determining reading practices during this period is notoriously challenging because of the absence of reflective accounts by readers. By examining commonplace books we see readers working with two books simultaneously, making editorial choices while excerpting and changing the way certain sections are written. However, in this case, what is most striking is how closely the commonplace author has stuck to the texts he is copying. The production of this commonplace book is a concerted act of concentration, reproducing the contents of detailed, lengthy printed works with very little amendment. Reading practices varied during the early modern period just as they do today. Commonplace books were sometimes the result of a drive for self-improvement. The eighteenth-century idea of the 'self' had not yet been fully formed, but in the seventeenth century reading was thought to be a good way of exercising the mind, and transcribing notes was a way of enhancing that process. However, the commonplace book is very different from a journal, in which authors strove for improvement through self-reflection, and from the notebook in which day to day thoughts and notes might be inserted. Unlike the journal, the commonplace book contains little reference to the passing of time. It is often impossible to say how many sittings the notes took to write or the time interval between sessions. The role of the commonplace author is also different in that he does not usually push himself forward in the text, rather, allowing the authors' voices whose work he is reading to dominate. Despite the lack of direct clues, some conclusions can be drawn about the commonplacers themselves through an analysis of their reading.

The manuscript commonplace book reproduced here is held at the British Library, part of number 6494 in Harleian Manuscript collections. It contains 33 folio pages, with 61 numbered paragraphs all written in the same hand. Robert Harley assembled his library in 1704 when he purchased over six hundred manuscripts from the collection of Sir Simonds D'Ewes (died 1650). However, 6494 was not part of this original core of manuscripts because it was produced over 20 years after the death of D'Ewes (see below for dating evidence). The rest of the collection, assembled in the 1710s and 1720s by Harley and his son, Edward, consisted of items obtained from auctions held in England and in continental Europe. 6494 is a miscellaneous collection of documents, including notes on the law, lists of church benefices, Francis Mason's notes on astronomy from the 1590s, a translation of Aesop's fables, an *Elogium* of Thomas Aquinas, the relation of a journey into the west of England, by an anonymous author, a tract on usury, a letter from a Roman Catholic to his Protestant friend, a treatise on the art of courtship and another on the soul. None of the other items in 6494 are in the same hand as the commonplace book. The commonplace book appears in the catalogue to the Harleian Manuscripts as item 14:

'collections relating the West Indies, the Affairs of Europe & several historical occurrences in England'.[1]

The handwriting is mostly legible and the document undamaged but it contains many contractions, which encouraged me to produce a modern version of the commonplace book. It reveals the topics that were important to a seventeenth-century reader and the editorial choices he made in taking notes, but until now these notes have not been placed in their proper context. A modern edition is timely because the Early English Books Online database, and the full text searches that it permits, allows the marrying of the extracts with the books from which these notes originally came.

The books used by the commonplace author were mostly easy to identify using the search engines on Early English Books Online, although it proved more challenging to pinpoint particular editions. Dating evidence was used as a guide. In paragraph 19 (footnote 136), the commonplace author wrote that the Reformation took place 140 years previously. This was not something derived from the original text, but was inserted by the compiler, and must have referred to the period when he was writing. Therefore, the time of writing was around either 1647 or 1676, depending on whether the date of Reformation was estimated from Luther's *Ninety-Five Theses* or Henry VIII's break with the Church of Rome as fixed by the Act of Appeals. The latter date is confirmed as one section of the text was copied from a book published in 1679 with no

---

[1] *A Catalogue of the Harleian Collection of Manuscripts*, Volume 2, p. 7076.

earlier editions. The evidence suggests 1679-80 as the date of the commonplace book.

The identity of the commonplace author remains as yet unknown. There are no definitive clues within the text as to gender, although the weight of probability is that it is a man. In light of this, for ease, I will refer to the commonplace author as 'he'. The choice of books from which notes were taken suggest certain areas of interest, some of which are typical of an educated man of the seventeenth century, while others are more unusual. The text is continuous and there is no attempt to categorise the diverse information into themes by using headings or an index. Throughout the commonplace book the choice of extracts reflects an interest in the unusual, even the bizarre. Religion is also a focus but the classical authors were ignored, in contrast to many commonplace books of the time; moreover the compiler omitted to copy a number of classical references found in the original books that he was working from. He was interested in stories of fabulous creatures in the Americas, descriptions of Luther's graphic cartoons satirising the Pope and accounts of the iconoclasm committed on the 'Eleanor Cross' at Cheapside in London.

The reader's interests initially took him across the Atlantic. Much of this section was taken from Samuel Purchas's monumental five-volume work *Purchas, His Pilgrims* first published in London in 1625. Purchas was a Church of England clergyman and a member of the Virginia Company. He took over the mantle of Richard Hakluyt in gathering together travel narratives documenting the forays of English merchants and sailors around the world. Purchas spent about twenty years gathering manuscript, printed and oral accounts and tying them together with anti-Catholic editorial polemic. The interests reflected in the notes derived from Purchas are of curious stories, such as reports of mermaids. There is no unifying theme of chronology, geography or individual traveller. The commonplace author indicated that he believed that individual sailors' and nations' stories are universal by removing their specific names and thoughts from his version of their stories. He ignored a comment by Purchas that credited wondrous creatures to God's creation, which may suggest that the interest of the author lay in the scientific rather than providential approach to the natural world. Determining the origin of this early section of the commonplace book (paragraphs 1-14) proved particularly challenging because Purchas's work is derived from a number of previously published works and many later authors used Purchas's work as a basis for their own. When undertaking searches on Early English Books Online, multiple possibilities presented themselves and all of these have been noted in the accompanying notes and bibliography. The commonplace author was most likely working from an edition of Purchas because his book is the unifying source that covers the entire section.

Another interest is the history of the continental Reformation, with some reference also to the return of Catholicism to England under Mary. There is a fascination with ceremony, and information about Catholic rituals and beliefs was copied without any additional comment. All the books from which notes on the Reformation were taken are texts written by Protestants and so consequently make their own judgements about Catholicism. The commonplacer does not contradict or comment on any of these opinions. John Sleidan (or Johannes Sleidanus), one important source, was an early historian of the Reformation from Luxembourg and his work is the source of the notes in paragraphs 15 to 35. While undertaking diplomatic work, which included periods in England and at the Council of Trent, Sleiden collected materials for his history. Although he finished writing his history just before his death, Sleiden was unable to afford to print it and died in poverty in 1556. Denouncing corruption within the Catholic Church, Sleiden's polemic was violently partisan with accounts of the suppression of particular ideas, as well as the sinfulness of Popes featuring strongly. By undertaking a textual comparison, it becomes clear that the commonplace text is closest to the earliest English translation, the 1560 edition produced by John Day. Day was committed to the evangelical cause and used his role as printer and bookseller to promote this during the 1540s. Later, Day used his connections with members of the continental printing and bookselling trades to attract lucrative works to England such as that by Sleiden. In 1563 the success of such ventures allowed Day to produce his most famous work: Foxe's *Acts and Monuments*, better known as the *Book of Martyrs*. For an author as concerned with Catholicism and martyrdom in England as the commonplace author obviously is, the omission of notes from Foxe, the perhaps second most widely read text during this period after the Bible, seems striking. Perhaps he already owned a copy of Foxe or was so familiar with its contents that he felt it unnecessary to take notes from it.

Sleiden's book shares a common theme with the next book used by the commonplace author: they are both concerned with the ritual and performance of authority. The next sequence of notes is taken from Richard Baker's 1643 volume, *A Chronicle of the Kings of England* (paragraphs 36-47). Baker was a defender of the Caroline court, engaging in polemical debate with William Prynne whose savage treatise, *Histriomastix,* characterised the court as popish and slandered Henrietta Maria, Charles II's wife. Baker's *magnum opus*, his history of the kings of England, dedicated to the young Prince Charles (the future Charles II), was written while in the Fleet prison for debt, where he spent the last ten years of his life. The book went through five reprints in England alone between 1665 and 1680 and was also translated into Dutch. Although now considered defective as historical scholarship, during the late seventeenth century its influence was unchallenged. Its popularity was due to the appealing nature of its narrative - a key attraction for the commonplace author. He copied extraordinary stories designed to provoke both shock and laughter, such as that of the horrific burial of William the Conqueror whose corpse exploded when the coffin lid was closed. But notes taken from both Baker's and Sleiden's works reflect an interest in formal ceremonial, in the orders of aristocratic hierarchy and in the source of royal and religious authority.

But the compiler was also interested in the vicissitudes of worldly power and the downfall of eminent men and women. One vivid story taken from Baker recounted the execution of Mary Queen of Scots. It contrasted the calmness and dignity with which she went to her death with the wrangling over Elizabeth I's culpability in agreeing to her execution. One of the smallest extracts from a single book is taken from James I's account of the execution of Henry Garnet, Superior of the Jesuits in England (paragraph 49). James's account of the Gunpowder Plot was first published in 1605, but the commonplace author definitely used the later version because Garnet died in 1606 and so the extract about his death only appeared in the 1679 edition. During the period when the commonplace author was writing there was a heightened fear of Catholics following the Popish plot and the Exclusion crisis of the late 1670s. These events formed the backdrop for the commonplace author's interest in the threat that Catholicism might pose.

The legality and rituals of kingship are noted from Nathaniel Bacon's *A Continuation of a Historical Discourse* of 1651 (paragraphs 50-53 and 58). There is also a 1689 version, but the notes are significantly closer to that of 1651. The commonplace author writing at the end of the 1670s was only a generation removed from the turmoil of the Civil War. As fear of Catholicism again threatened the stability of the realm, readers turned to books written during the Civil War period for answers to questions about their future. Bacon was a supporter of the Long Parliament and his cynical views on monarchy come through strongly in his writing. During his lifetime the book was highly regarded and his contemporary, Richard Baxter, called it one of the most significant works of the Civil War era. Drawing heavily on the notes of John Selden (indeed some consider Bacon the editor rather than the author), the work showed the shaky grounds on which many English kings had claimed the throne, and explained the political and legal contortions that the nation had gone through in order to acknowledge their rights. His overall thesis is that Parliament was justified in its attack on Charles I. The book went through a secret reprinting in 1672, and again in 1682 during the Exclusion crisis. Charles II was very worried by its popularity and its printer, John Starkey, was prosecuted twice for distributing it. Hundreds of copies were publicly burnt.[2]

    Moving away from royalty and religion, the compiler took notes from John Stow's very popular *Survey of London* (paragraph 54). Stow was an avid collector of manuscripts and his role as an historian is significant, but it was his authorship of the *Survey of London* that has defined him; the work has remained constantly in print since the first edition in 1598. Stow's personal knowledge of London and his interest in pageantry pervade the book, but it was not a section on pageantry and display that was chosen by the commonplacer, but one discussing Roman archaeological discoveries in Spitalfields in 1576. Perhaps the author lived close by. Continuing with the theme of London, the commonplace author moved on to James Howell's *Londinopolis* of 1657, to take notes about the mayor, William Walworth, and his capture of the rebel Wat Tyler (paragraphs 55-57). After this, at paragraph 58, the notes revert to a previous book, that of Bacon. This is an intriguing example of his reading practices where, after notes were taken from one book, the commonplacer then swapped to another book and then back to the first. The topics do not obviously overlap, although the Wat Tyler

---

[2] *CSP Domestic, 1682*, 263, 608; *CSP Domestic, 1677-8*, 406, 409; *Oxford Dictionary of National Biography* (2004), Nathaniel Bacon.

extract might be seen as continuing the theme of challenges to monarchical authority.

James Howell is the only author to whose books the commonplacer refers twice. In paragraph 59, in another dramatic change of subject, he takes notes from Howell's *Epistolae Holianae* of 1650 about the spa waters at Bath. The section copied is a scientific treatise on the natural heat of the waters rather than a discussion of their medicinal value. Coincidentally, like Richard Baker, James Howell was imprisoned in the Fleet for debt at the time of writing his work, and like Nathaniel Bacon, he was in contact with the great lawyer and patron, John Selden. Howell's writing was an attempt to find a moderate way through the religious and political turmoil of his time, but although he leant more towards the Royalist side, he was not rewarded with preferment at the Restoration and instead made his living from literary publications.

Paragraph 60 is the only mystery in the commonplace book, an extract for which no source has been identified among printed works published in England. Possibly this section comes from a manuscript treatise, or a translation of a Latin or other foreign language work. The final paragraph of the book represents another radical departure in topic, covering the history and geography of Palestine that was taken from Gerard Mercator's book *Historia Mundi* (the 1635 English edition)

These works are all copied very closely but they also reveal both calculated and accidental changes made by the commonplace author. There are editorial choices throughout that might tell us something about his identity. He changed accounts written in the first person (especially in the section from Purchas) into the third person. He rendered these accounts in the passive voice. He seemed reluctant to copy someone else's story directly, but rather tried to make it his own or, at the very least, to make it universal. From the sections taken from Bacon's book, the commonplace author consistently ignored the classical and legal references included by Bacon.

There are also accidental omissions, especially when the author is copying long lists of information. One example is in footnote 374 where a list of Eleanor crosses comes from Howell's *Londinopolis*. The place name 'Waltham' is omitted completely from the list, surely an oversight. However, in the same list, 'West Cheap' in the original is changed to 'Cheapside' in the commonplace text. This seems to be a deliberate amendment reflecting an updated usage.

Not every change is an omission; in many places the author added information. This is often to clarify a passage in which the original is not clear about dates, places or names. This suggests that the commonplace author expected to make use of his notes at a later date and wanted their meaning to be absolutely clear. Other examples in footnotes 290 and 299 refer to blanks left in the manuscript. The commonplace author clearly intended to identify the name of the missing county and add it later. Either he forgot to do so, or could not find the information.

One change of spelling appears throughout the manuscript. In the original, where the word 'been' or 'beene' appears, the commonplace author always rendered it 'bin'. The author was not copying letter for letter the words in the text that he had read. He might read a sentence, process it, think it through, and then write it down. In his own accent, in his own head, the word 'been' sounds more like 'bin'. Or perhaps he was taught that the correct spelling was 'bin'. Inconsistency of spelling is ubiquitous during this period, and the authors of the original works are certainly not consistent, so I would argue that the consistent use of 'bin' reflects the normal usage by the commonplacer.

To assign authorship to the commonplace book is to enter the realms of speculation. But the reading practices revealed here offer a possible suggestion. The largest single extract copied (paragraphs 15 to 35) is taken from the John Day edition of John Sleidan's work on the history of the Reformation and is obviously of key interest to our author. Even though these passages comprise a small part of Sleidan's magisterial work and the commonplacer was interested in other authors, it raises the possibility that he might be George Bohun, the translator of the next edition of Sleidan in 1689.[3] Bohun's personal history certainly chimes with the interests revealed here. The son of a Church of England minister from New House, Keresley, Coventry, Bohun decided not to follow in his father's footsteps and instead moved to London to pursue a mercantile career. George was overshadowed by Ralph, his more successful elder brother. Ralph did enter the church, went to Oxford and became tutor to John Evelyn's children. Evelyn became his patron throughout his life. George, also an Anglican, fell

---

[3] R.G. Thorne, ed., *History of Parliament: Commons 1790-1820* (London, 1986); *Oxford Dictionary of National Biography* (2004), George Bohun.

foul of Coventry's Presbyterians by presenting St. Michael's church (later the cathedral) with two great candlesticks. He had trading interests in overseas companies such as the African Company, which might explain a concern with Purchas's accounts of the Azores and America. Ralph too, had an interest in travel and science; while at Oxford in 1671 he published a treatise on hurricanes. When he married in 1681, George was living in Cheapside, chiming with the commonplacer's interest in accounts of the city by Stow and Howell, and his notes on Cheapside. Later in 1690, when his younger brother died, George inherited family property in Spitalfields. Family connections in the area might have encouraged an interest in the Roman archaeological remains found there a century earlier. Bohun subsequently became the Tory MP for Coventry and a lieutenant of the city. He was buried in a family vault in St. Michael's. If he is indeed the author of the commonplace book, then he compiled it in his late thirties and at the peak of his mercantile career, and when he was preparing to establish himself with Tory grandees and to manoeuvre into political power. This identification remains highly speculative, however. The antimonarchical flavour of his extracts from Bacon do not fit easily with the sentiments of a Tory.

Editorial Note:

In this modern edition I have expanded the numerous contractions and modernised spelling and punctuation except in the case of personal and place names. I have also tried to retain the spirit of the original and have not modernised idioms or sentence structure. My task was to tidy the manuscript rather than rewrite it. This means that the voices of both the author of the published work *and* of the commonplace author come through in this version.

Bibliography of works on commonplacing and early modern reading practices

David Allan, *Commonplace Books and Reading in Georgian England* (Cambridge, 2010)

Jennifer Andersen & Elizabeth Sauer, eds., *Books and Readers in Early Modern England: Material Studies* (Philadelphia, PN., 2002)

Sabrina Alcorn Baron, ed., *The Reader Revealed* (Washington, DC, 2001)

Peter Beal, 'Notions in Garrison: The Seventeenth-Century Commonplace Book,' in *New Ways of Looking at Old Texts: Papers of the Renaissance English Text Society, 1985–1991*, ed. W. Speed Hill (Binghamton, N.Y.: Medieval & Renaissance Texts and Studies, with Renaissance English Text Society, 1993) vol. 107, pp. 131–47.

Ronald Bedford, Lloyd Davis & Phillipa Kelly, *Early Modern Autobiography: Theories, genres, Practices* (Ann Arbor, MI., 2006)

Ann Blair, 'Note Taking as a Form of Transmission', *Critical Enquiry*, vol. 31, no. 1 (Autumn 2004), pp. 85-107.

Stephen Colclough, 'Recovering the Reader: Commonplace Books and Diaries as Sources of Reading Experience', *Publishing History*, 44 (1998), pp. 5-37

Stephen Colclough, *Consuming Texts: Readers and Reading Communities 1695-1870* (Basingstoke, 2007)

Lucia Dacome: 'Noting the Mind: Commonplace Books and the Pursuit of the Self in Eighteenth-Century

Britain', *Journal of the History of Ideas*, vol. 65, no. 4 (Oct, 2004), pp. 603-625.

Ian Green, *Print and Protestantism in Early Modern England* (Oxford, 2000)

Earle Havens, *Commonplace Books: A History of Manuscripts and Printed Books from Antiquity to the Present* (Lebanon, NH., 2002)

David McKitterick, *Print, Manuscript and the Search for Order, 1450-1830* (Cambridge, 2003)

Ann Moss, *Printed Commonplace Books and the Structuring of Renaissance Thought* (Oxford, 1996)

Jennifer Richards, 'Useful Books: Reading Vernacular Regimens in Sixteenth-Century England', *Journal of the History of Ideas*, vol. 73, no. 2 (April 2012), pp. 247-271.

Isabel Rivers, *Books and their Readers in Eighteenth-Century England* (Leicester, 1982)

Isabel Rivers, *Books and their Readers in Eighteenth-Century England: New Essays* (Leicester, 2001)

Kevin Sharpe, *Reading Revolutions: The Politics of Reading in Early Modern England* (New Haven, CT., 2000)

Kevin Sharpe and Steven Zwicker, eds., *Reading, Society, and Politics in Early Modern England* (Cambridge, 2003)

W.H. Sherman, *John Dee: The Politics of Reading and Writing in the English Renaissance* (Amherst, MA., 1990)

Adam Smyth, *Autobiography in Early Modern England* (Cambridge, 2010)

D. R. Woolf, *Reading History in Early Modern England* (Cambridge, 2000)

List of Paragraphs[4]

Paragraph number: Topic:

1	Tortoises
2	Brazil
3	Panama
4	Azores
5	Bermudas
6	Newfoundland
7	Newfoundland
8	Moose, Possum and other animals
9	Brazilian Parrots
10	Mermaid
11	Dolphins
12	Swordfish
13	Solomon Islands
14	Penguin
15	Father Landre of Paris
16	Francis I
17	Francis I
18	Calvin's Works

---

[4] This list will help the reader navigate through the modern edition. There is no contents page or index in the commonplace book itself.

19	Mary's reign
20	–
21	–
22	–
23	–
24	Council of Trent
25	Francis I
26	Henry II
27	Peter Aloise
28	Paul III
29	Council of Trent
30	Maximilian
31	Charles the Wise
32	Reformation
33	Religious debates, Cardinal Pole
34	Council of Trent
35	Cardinal Pole
36	Edward the Confessor
37	Richard I
38	Henry VII
39	William the Conqueror
40	Mary Queen of Scots
41	Mary Queen of Scots

42	Duke of Norfolk
43	Mary Queen of Scots
44	Penance, 1417
45	Thomas Arundel
46	Henry VIII's wives
47	Edward III
48	Peter of Savoy
49	Henry Garnet
50	Henry VII
51	Mary I
52	Reigning monarchs without title
53	Female monarchs
54	Archaeology at Spitalfields
55	Jack Straw
56	Eleanor crosses
57	Use of *Custos Regni*
58	Privy Council
59	Medicinal Waters at Bath
60	Marriage of clergy
61	Canaan

Modern Edition: Harley 6494 (14)

[5]The tortoises[6] are shaped like a crab and have four fins; they are as large commonly as three or four men can carry and the upper part of them has a great thick shell. They weigh nearly two hundredweight. The flesh that cleaves to the inside of it when roasted is excellent meat, almost like beef marrow, yet it is the kind of meat that cannot be absolutely called 'fish'. It keeps most of its flesh in the sea and feeds upon sea-grass like a cow, in the bottom of the bays, which made the Spanish Friars, at first, have some scruple to eat them on a Friday.[7] In colour and taste the flesh

---

[5] Taken from Samuel Purchas, *Purchas his pilgrimes In fiue bookes*[...](London, 1625), p. 1800. From manuscript version of Richard Norwood's 'The Description of the Summer Islands' or from the now lost *A Plotte or Map of Bermudas or the Summer Islands made by RN* (entered into Stationer's Company 19 Jan 1621-2). Almost identical to the Purchas version is John Speed, *A prospect of the most famous parts of the vvorld*[..]. (London, 1631), p. 43. Samuel Clarke, *A true and faithful account of the four chiefest plantations of the English in America to wit, of Virginia, New-England, Bermudus, Barbados*[...] (London, 1670), pp. 20-21. G. H. *Memorabilia mundi, or, Choice memoirs of the history and description of the world by G.H* (London, 1670), pp. 47-51. John Smith also used part of Norwood's description of Bermuda, although not this extract, in his *Generall Historie of Virginia*[...] (London, 1624), pp. 177-89.

[6] Actually sea turtles, see later comments about being found at sea. Norwood says elsewhere in his 'Description' that he has chosen to write about turtles because their 'affinitie and resemblance with Fishes, Beastes and Fowles shall serve in stead of a Historie of them all'. *The Journal of Richard Norwood, surveyor of Bermuda*, ed. W. F. Craven and W. B. Hayward (New York, 1945), p. lxxxiii.

[7] 'It keeps most of its flesh in the sea and feeds upon sea-grass like a cow, in the bottom of the bays, which made the Spanish Friars at first, have some scruple to eat them on a Friday': this sentence does not appear in other printed versions. This detail suggests either that the

is like the most tender bits of veal, and even the very guts and maw are good meat for they are exceedingly fat, and make as good tripe as any ox. The upper shell is harder than horn, it has also a shell on its belly, less hard and when boiled it becomes soft like the gristles of beef and is good meat. They are like fowl in the smallness of the heads and necks, which are wrinkled like a turkey's, but are white and not so sharp billed and they breed their young ones from eggs which they lay. They resemble beasts, in that their flesh is like veal, and they feed upon grass. They can survive no longer under water than they hold their breath, which the old ones will do for a long time, but the young ones being chased to and fro, cannot stay for more than two or three minutes without coming up to breathe. They are in great plenty around the Bermudas, where they spend the spring time and part of the summer, but where they are the rest of the year is unknown.[8] Shortly after their appearing the male and female (moved by the heat of generation) do couple which there they call 'cooting'. They continue doing this for three days during which time they will hardly separate even if a boat comes near them. Not long after, the she tortoise comes up by night upon a sandy bay and farther up than the tide line, she digs a hole with her fins in the sand two feet deep, and there coming up for several nights, lays her eggs[9]

---

commonplace author has spoken to someone who witnessed the event themselves or has derived this description from another, unknown manuscript source.

[8] In Purchas, this sentence appears earlier, after 'gristles of beef and is good meat'.

[9] 'about half a Bushell' appears in Purchas, *Purchas, His Pilgrims;* Speed, *A Prospect*; Clarke, *A True and Faithful Account*; and G.H., *Memorabilia Mundi*, but appears crossed out in the commonplace book.

at several times and at each time covers them with sand very curiously, so that the place can hardly be found: the eggs are as big as turkey's,[10] and as round as a ball. She lays about four hundred in all, so leaving them is not careful of the Succession; At the day appointed to the procreation of these creatures, there creeps out many tortoises, like Pismires out of an anthill,[11] and they do this only by the sun's heat, without any help from the adults: so that is by the mere guidance of God (all other means being as yet unknown) that they are produced. The she tortoise does not come to them any more, and yet in likelihood they do not remain long in the sand after they are hatched, because (as before is said) they cannot live without breathing. Some fishes will devour the young ones when they are no bigger than a man's hand; they grow slowly and seem to live for a long time; they will sleep on the top of the water, and slept often on the land before people came to the country. They will live for eighteen or twenty days out of the water,[12] and that without eating any meat, yet they will mourn and pine away the

---

[10] In Purchas, *Purchas, His Pilgrims;* Speed, *A Prospect*; Clarke, *A True and Faithful Account*; and G.H., *Memorabilia Mundi,* this appears as 'the bignesse of a Hennes Egge'. The reason for this change by the commonplace author is unclear, perhaps to make the size sound more dramatic, and make a comparison connected with the Americas, Turkeys being an indigenous species.

[11] 'She lays about four hundred in all, so leaving them is nothing careful of the Succession; At the day appointed to the procreation of these creatures, there creeps out many tortoises, like Pismires out of an anthill': this clause does not appear in the printed extracts. This vivid description suggests either that the commonplace author has witnessed this event for themselves or has spoken to someone who has, or has derived this description from another, unknown MS source.

[12] 'some three weeks' in Purchas, *Purchas, His Pilgrims*.

while. Being on the land, and turned upon their backs, they cannot recover themselves without some help, so when they come on shore to lay their eggs, they are easily taken, as also when they are cooting. But otherwise they are taken by making a great light in a boat, to which they will sometimes swim, and seldom shun; so that a man standing there ready with a staff in his hand, which hath a socket at one end of it, within is a piece of iron smaller than a man's finger 4 square 6 inches long[13] and sharp-pointed, with a line fastened to the other end. He strikes this iron into the upper shell of the tortoise and it sticks so fast, that after it has tired itself with swimming to and fro, it is taken by it. They remain alive for twenty-four hours after the head is cut off, so that if the flesh be cut with a knife it will suffice eighty men at a meal, especially if it is a she tortoise, for she will have enough eggs for fifty hungry men for a dinner.[14]

2.[15] X Upon the coast of Brazil in the West Indies and in all other countries in those parts that are hot[16] there is a small

---

[13] 'six inches long' does not appear in Purchas, *Purchas, His Pilgrims*.

[14] 'it will suffice eighty men at a meal, especially if it is a she tortoise, for she will have enough eggs for fifty hungry men for a dinner': last sentence not included in other printed accounts. Purchas version adds 'if you cut the flesh with a Knife, or touch it, it will tremble and shrinke away.'

[15] Purchas, *Purchas, His Pilgrims*, pp. 1386-87. Also possible as a source is Richard Hawkins, *The observations of Sir Richard Havvkins Knight, in his voiage into the South Sea. Anno Domini 1593* (London, 1622), pp. 78-80. Hawkins's and Purchas's accounts are rendered in the first person.

precious worm[17] called by the English 'Arters',[18] and by the Spaniards 'Brown'. They will enter into the planks of ships, and especially where there are rivers of fresh water, for it is the common opinion that they are bred in fresh water, and brought into the sea with the current of the rivers. But the mariners by their experience have found that they breed in the wide seas in all hot climates, especially near the Equinoctial Line. For a ship lying long under the water and near the Line and a shallop being towed at the ship's stern came to be cleansed in Brazil. She was found to be covered with these worms as big as a man's little finger under the water line, on the outside of the plank. They were not fully covered but half the thickness of their body, like a jelly, wrought into the plank like a goudge.[19] These worms put everyone in danger, if a ship is not sheathed, for they enter

---

[16] 'in the West Indies and in all other countries in those parts that are hot' is an addition in the commonplace book, not present in either Hawkins, *Observations*, or Purchas, *Purchas, His Pilgrims*.

[17] Also known as the 'terodo' worm.

[18] In Hawkins *Observations*, and Purchas, *Purchas, His Pilgrims*, the word 'English' is rendered 'us'. Does this mean that the commonplace author does not consider himself 'English'? More likely, he wanted to clarify the ambiguous pronoun, showing he intended to return later to his notes.

[19] Here a section that appears in Hawkins, *Observations*, or Purchas, *Purchas, His Pilgrims* is omitted. The passage appears thus in Hawkins: 'And naturall reason (in my judgment confirmeth this; for creatures bread and nourished in the Sea, comming into fresh water die; as those actually bred in Ponds or fresh Rivers die presently, if they come into Salt water. But some man may say; this fayleth in some Fishes and Beasts. Which I must confesse to be true; but these eyther are part terrestryall, and part aquatile, as the Maremaide, Sea Horse and other of that kind, or have their breeding in the fresh, and growth or continuall nourishment in the Salt water as the Salmond and others of that kinde'. p. 79.

into a hole no bigger than a small Spanish needle, and their holes become ordinarily greater than a man's finger and the thicker the plank is the greater the worms grow. Some seamen tell us that they have seen many ships eaten like this,[20] so that the most of their planks under water became like honey-combs, and especially those between wind and water if they were not sheathed. It was impossible that they could have swum into the planks, in fact the entering of them cannot be discerned.[21] Therefore all who plan long voyages should prevent the great mischief by sheathing their ships.

The manner of sheathing of ships is done in many ways. In Spain and Portugal some sheath their ships with lead, which besides the cost and weight, although they use the thinnest sheet of lead that is to be seen anywhere, yet it is not durable but subject to many casualties; Another manner is used with double planks after the manner of furring, which is little better than that with lead: for besides the weight it lasts only a short time because the worm quickly passes through the one and then the other. A third manner of sheathing hath been used among some with fine canvas, which is of small continuance,[22] and so is not to be regarded. The fourth prevention, which now is most popular, is to burn the upper plank till it looks like a coal, and after to pitch it, this is not

---

[20] In the Hawkins, *Observations*, this appears as 'I have seene many shippes so eaten'. Another example of the first person being rendered into the third person.

[21] In Hawkins, *Observations* and Purchas, *Purchas His Pilgrims* the clause is added 'the most of them being small as the head of a Pinne'.

[22] 'of small continuance', i.e. does not last long.

bad. In China (as is reported)[23] they use a certain varnish, in manner of an artificial Pitch, with which they trim the outside of their ships. It is said to be so durable that neither worm nor water can pierce it, nor has the sun any power against it. Some have devised a certain Pitch mingled with glass and other ingredients, which is beaten into powder with which if the ship is pitched, it is said, that the worm that touches it, dies. But yet by experience this has not been useful[24] but the most approved manner of sheathing which was invented by Sir John Hawkins[25] and is nowadays in use in England and that is with thin boards, half an inch thick, the thinner the better, and elm is better than oak for it does not spilt, it endures better under water, and moulds better to the Ship's side: the invention of the [...]That is incorporated between the plank and the sheathing is that indeed which avails, for without it many planks were not sufficient to hinder the entrance of the worm. The manner is this: before the sheathing board is nailed on,[26] the inner side of it is smeared all over with tar, half a finger thick, and upon the tar another half finger thick of hair, such as the white-

---

[23] In the original by Richard Hawkins this is rendered 'as I have been informed'. The change shows that the commonplace author wants to make a distinction between information verified in print and that which he/she perceives to be hearsay.

[24] In the Hawkins, *Observations* this appears as 'I have not heard that it hath beene usefull', again removing the first person narrative.

[25] This is the father of the author of the original text printed in 1622, rendered 'my father' in the original.

[26] This section appears in active voice in the Hawkins and Purchas versions, suggesting that the commonplace reader is reporting this as a theoretical method rather than the subjective experience of one voyager.

lymers[27] use. And so nail it on, the nails not a span distance one from another, and the thicker they are driven the better; Some hold opinion that the tar kills the worm, others that the worm passing the sheathing and seeking a way through, the hair and the tar so involve that she is choked therewith, which is thought to be most probable. This way experience has taught to be the best and of least cost.[28]

3. Pearls are found in diverse parts of the world, such as the East Indian Sea, in the South Sea, in the West Indies in the Straits of Magellan, and in the Scottish Sea; those found near the Poles are not perfect, but are of a thick dull colour, whereas those found near the Line are most Orient and transparent. The curious call it 'that water', and the best are clear white shining, with fiery flames. Those of East India have the best reputation though as good are found in the West Indian and in the South Seas. Those in the Magellan Straits are both small and of a bad colour, being but seed pearl, as are those in the Scottish Sea.[29] The fishing for pearls both in the East and West Indies are much alike, and that is, with small barks, in which there are 4, 5, 6 or 8 persons,[30] expert swimmers and divers, which through the

---

[27] A white wash used to paint houses.

[28] Original refers to 'this manner of sheathing was invented by my father' i.e. John Hawkins. This is omitted in these notes.

[29] In the original, this section appears after the description of fishing for pearls. In the original the information preceding concerns Hawkins' ship the *Dainty* and some of its problems.

[30] 'negroes' in Hawkins. Perhaps the commonplacer is suggesting that anyone can fish for pearls, and therefore there is potential for English settlers to make money.

passage of time, use and continual practice have learned to hold their breath long under water, for the better achieving their work. Throwing themselves into the sea, with certain instruments of their art, they go to the bottom and seek the banks of the oysters in which the pearls are engendered and with force and art remove them from their fixed foundation in which they spend more or less time, according to the resistance and the firmness of the ground, they put them into a bag which is tied under their arms, and when it is full, up they come and put them into the barks and so down again for more, till they be laden. Then they go ashore, and open the oysters and take out the pearls; they use under the uppermost part of the circuit of the oyster in ranks and proportions, under a certain part which is of many pleats and folds, called 'the ruff', for the similarity it has to a ruff. The pearls increase in size, as they are nearer to the end or joint of the oyster; the meat of those which have these pearls are milky and unwholesome to eat.

As for the generation of pearls and their breeding in oysters, found (as is said) growing within the shell under the ruff of the oyster, some say of the dew, which is held to be but some old Philosophers' conceit[31] for it cannot be made out as in any way probable, how the dew should come into the oyster. And if it were true, then doubtless there should be

---

[31] Hawkins hints that Pliny has an idea about the origin of pearls that has now been discredited. Somehow the commonplace author has introduced the idea of 'Dew' being a cause. Hawkins does not mention this. Purchas does not discuss the origin of pearls at all. This is therefore an example of knowledge from another manuscript source or from the commonplacer's own knowledge being integrated into the note-taking.

pearls in the English oysters, as in those of the East and West Indies, because being in shallower water, and not fastened to the bottom of the rocks, as the others are but those oysters were by the creator made to bring forth this rare production all their shells being (to look like) pearl itself and the other pearls found in the oysters and muscles had in some parts of England and in the Straits aforesaid are engendered out of the fatness of the fish. And in the very substance of the fish so that in some oysters and muscles have been found 20 or more in several parts of the fish, and these not perfect in colour, roundness or clearness as those found in the Pearl-Oyster which are ever perfect in all those three qualities, in colour and clearness being like the sun in his rising and therefore called Oriental, and not (as is supposed) because out of the East; for they are as well found in the West, and no way inferior unto those of the East Indies. The choice pearls such as are called Unions, because there are two found together, round and large, and sized alike, and any other that are great and round, are of high value and estimation.[32] But the greatest that have of late ages been discovered, was a pearl found in those Islands of Pearls, which being many and which are in the West Indies, and lie along the Coast, beginning eight miles West South-West from Panama, and run to the Southwards, near 30 Leagues. Most of them are inhabited and those which are have some Negros, slaves to the Spaniards, of which many are employed in fishing for pearls. This pearl was called La Peregrina, for the rareness of it, being as big as the pommel of an ordinary Spanish poniard; Philip II, King of Spain gave it to his daughter Isabella Clara Eugenia, wife to

---

[32] This is the point at which the notes rejoin the Purchas/Hawkins texts.

Albertus, Arch-Duke of Austria, and Governor of the Spanish Netherlands.[33]

4.[34] The Islands of the Azores are situated in the Atlantic or Western Ocean, and do stand between 37 and 40 Degrees and 400 Leagues distant from England. They are in number seven. That is Tercera, St Mary, St Michael, St George, Gratiosa, Pico and Fayal: There are yet two islands more, called Flores and Cuervo, which are not comprehended under the name of Azores but yet at this day are under the Government of the same, so that they are accounted nine islands.[35] The name Azores was given to these islands by the Portuguese, of a kind of hawks, called by them Azores or Goshawks,[36] because in their first discovery of them, they found many Goshawks there although today there are not any there to be found. They are also called the Flemish Islands, the Netherlanders challenging that they were first

---

[33] Hawkins describes this as 'Flanders', perhaps to deny the control exerted by the Spaniards.

[34] This section taken from Purchas only, p. 408. No printed version of this text exists anywhere else. Purchas has heavily edited Arthur Gorges' manuscript notes before publication, often interjecting his own views and information from Linschoten. He has removed a long preface to Prince Henry. The book was written in 1607 but concerns the Earl of Essex's failed voyage of 1597 to intercept the Spanish treasure fleet.

[35] In Purchas's version, the names of the Azores islands are listed as nine in number. The qualifying statement about the further two islands found in the reader's notes do not come from Purchas.

[36] The Latin name 'Acciptres' is also given in Purchas' version. Also omitted is a comment about Ortellius's naming of the islands.

discovered by the Merchants of Bruges in Flanders,[37] who found them uninhabited, abounding in woods, whither they sent colonies to people and cultivate them. Today some of their offspring in manners and behaviour are altogether like Netherlanders, and there is yet a river where these inhabit called Aribera los Flemingos, that is the Flemish River.[38] But in process of time, they yielded themselves as subjects to the Portuguese, who since inhabit and govern it, but afterward with them fell under the power of the Spaniard, anno 1580 and again returned to the obedience of the Crown of Portugal, anno 1640. John Duke of Braganza being seated on the throne by the name of John IV.[39] Among these islands Tercera is the chief, but so called by the Spaniards because it lies third island distant from the Spanish coast. It is between 15 and 16 miles in compass [.....] a great [.....] lands.[40]

It is as it were walled about with cliffs, but where any strand is there stands a fort. The chief town in it is called Angra, and this has a very strong fortress, called Brazil, and has under it a road[41] for ships to ride in. But a haven or safe port for all weathers, there is not one amongst all the nine

---

[37] Bruges in original and commonplace book 'Bridges'. In the manuscript the reader adds 'in Flanders', to remind himself where it is.

[38] This sentence does not appear in Purchas's original.

[39] Purchas's version only mentions usurpation by Spain, and does not give a date. The recovery of Portuguese independence and information about John Duke of Braganza occurred after the publication of Purchas's work. Perhaps this is common knowledge at the time at which the commonplace author is writing.

[40] The size of the island does not appear in the Purchas version.

[41] That is, sheltered water where ships can anchor.

islands. In the town the present King of Portugal's son, Alfonso, remains confined.[42] On one side of the island are two high hills, stretching into the sea, upon which stand two stone pillars where is a sentinel placed, that continually watches to see what ships are at sea and to advise the Flanders; for as many as he sees coming out of the West that is from the Spanish Indies, Brazil, Guiney, Capo Verde, and all other ways lying South or West, he sets up a flag upon the pillar in the West for every ship he decries, but if they be more than 5, then he sets up a great ancient,[43] betokening a whole fleet. The like he doth upon the other pillar which stands in the East, for such ships as come from Portugal or other places out of the East and North parts. These pillars may be seen in all places of the town, so that not one ship at sea makes toward the island, but it is presently known, both there and on all the whole island for the watch is not kept only upon those two hills, but also upon all corners and cliffs throughout the island, who advise the Governor and rulers what ships arrive. Upon the furthest corner in the sea stands a fort right against which is another that answers it, so that those two forts do shut and defend the open haven of the town, where the ships lie in the road: so that no ship can go in, or come forth without the licence and permission of those two forts. And in the town of Angra in the island, the Governor resides, and it is the metropolis and ruler over all the other islands, which are (as is said) these.

---

[42] This next section of notes are taken from a different part of Purchas's work: 'CHAP. XIIII.The description of the Ilands of Açores, or the Flemish Ilands, taken out of Linschoten, with certaine occurrents, and English acts.' p. 268

[43] That is, a large banner.

[44]St Michael which lies 9 Leagues South of the Tercera, and is 20 miles in compass; St Mary is 4 Leagues to the Southward of St Michael, and is about 10 or 12 miles in Compass; St George lies West North-West 3 Leagues from Tercera, and is 20 miles long, and 3 broad. These 3 islands were so called of those saints' names, upon whose days they were first discovered. Graciosa lies North North-West from Tercera about 3 Leagues, and is about 6 miles in Compass; Fayal lies West South-West 2 Leagues from St George and a half, 18 miles in compass. Pico is from Fayal South-East 1 League; from St George, South-West 2 Leagues, and from Tercera South-West and by West 4 Leagues, and is in compass 16 miles. Flores is 23 Leagues Westward from Tercera, and is about 7 miles about, the abundance of flowers that grow in it was the occasion of its name;[45] Cuervo, lies a mile from Flores, Northward and is a small island of 2 miles compass only, and was so called of the crows and ravens breeding therein. All these for temperature and fruitfulness, are equal to each other. But St Michael is

---

[44] This extract is not a direct copy from any single source, but rather an amalgamation of notes derived from reading three works: Sir Thomas Herbert, *Some yeares travels into divers parts of Asia and Afrique Describing especially the two famous empires, the Persian, and the great Mogull: weaved with the history of these later times as also, many rich and spatious kingdomes in the orientall India, and other parts of Asia; together with the adjacent iles. Severally relating the religion, language, qualities, customes, habit, descent, fashions, and other observations touching them. With a revivall of the first discoverer of America. Revised and enlarged by the author* (London, 1638) p. 186 and *Cosmographie in four bookes : containing the chorographie and historie of the whole vvorld, and all the principall kingdomes, provinces, seas and isles thereof* by Peter Heylyn (London, 1652). Purchas also discusses the same topic, p. 408.

[45] From here to the end of the paragraph is a copy of Purchas, p. 408

the greatest of them all, Tercera the strongest and St Mary's the nearest to the coast of Spain. The island Tercera lies under 39 Degrees, and in the same height that Lisbon lies, and is distant from thence lying right East and West 250 Spanish miles.

5.[46] The Bermudas, or Summer Islands were so called of Sir George Summers, who first made a full discovery and exact relation of them, and planted a colony. The first name Bermuda they received from one John Barmudaz, a Portuguese,[47] who first gave the English notice of them. They lie in the Western Ocean in the part of the world lately discovered and called America, or the New World, in 32 degrees and 25 minutes, which is also the same Latitude or elevation almost with the Madeiras, or rather somewhat more southward.[48] They are a line of broken islands and there are above 400 of them , in manner of an archipelago (at least if they maybe called islands, that lie how little [...] into the sea and by themselves) of small compass, some larger yet than others, as time and the sea hath worn from them and eaten his passage through, all now lying in the

---

[46] This extract on Bermuda taken from Samuel Purchas, p. 304. Purchas borrowed it from William Strachey's manuscript account of Gates's and Somers's voyage to Virginia. Also similar to Samuel Clarke, *A True and Faithful Account of the Four Chiefest Plantations of the English in America* (London, 1670), p. 10. It bears some similarities to Nicolas Sanson, *Cosmography and Geography in two parts* (London, 1682), p. 495, but the commonplace extract mirrors the Clarke version almost word for word and so is the most likely source.

[47] Clarke only gives surname of Bermudaz and not his nationality. Sanson gives his nationality as Spanish.

[48] 'somewhat more southward' added by the commonplace author.

figure of a croissant,[49] within the circuit of 7 Leagues at the most, albeit it is so that they sometimes were 13 or 14 Leagues. The main island, or greatest of them now, is 16 miles in length, the longest part of it lying East North-East, and West South-West, standing in 32 degrees and 20 minutes, in which is a Great Bay on the North Side in the North-West end, and many broken islands in it.[50] These islands are often afflicted and rent with tempests, thunderclaps, lightning, and rain, in the extremity of violence, some claps being as terrible as ever astonished mortal men and the rain falling with such force and darkness for the time, as if it would never be fair nor clear again, which tempests have so rent down the rocks and whurried[51] whole quarters of islands into the main sea (some 6 or 7 Leagues and is like to swallow them all) so as even in that distance from the shore, there is no small danger of them and with them of the storms continually raging among them, which once at the change of company of every moon (winter or summer) keep the unchangeable round and rather thunder than blow from every corner about them, sometimes for 50 hours together. There are one or two places (and scarce two except to such as know them well), the country being so environed with rocks, which makes it very strong, where shipping may safely come in, the passage being such as the most skilful mariners have not by chance or discovery been upon the

---

[49] This observation made by Sanson and not Clarke.

[50] This extract on the climate and navigability appears in Purchas only, neither Clarke nor Sanson include it. Purchas's version is similar also to the short pamphlet account given by Sylvester Jordain, *A Discovery of the Barmudas* (London, 1610).

[51] That is, broken.

like; and without a perfect knowledge and search made of these places it is impossible to bring in bable boats so much as of ten tun without apparent ruin,[52] albeit within there are many fair harbours, and room enough to entertain a Royal fleet with depth of water sufficient to ride in, and safe land-locked. The rocks in most places appear at low water, and not much covered at a full sea, for it ebbs and flows there not above 5 foot. The shore itself is (for the most part) a rock, and on one side only admits so much as hope of safety by many a League.[53] The soil of the whole island is one and the same, the mould dark red sandy, dry and incapable of European fruits, as at first was doubted; but the clearness of the air, as it commonly is and very temperate and the plants, corn, beasts and poultry transported thither out of England liking so well, as the former yields a far greater increase, and the other being fatter and better like than in England and if anything come not to the maturity as is requisite is because that a continual Spring seems to be there and though the trees do shed their leaves, yet are they always full of green.

6.[54] New-found-land is an island bordering upon the continent of America from which it is divided by the sea, so

---

[52] Purchas's account describes that 'I have often heard Captain Newport of George Summers say...'; this personal, first person extract removed by our commonplace author.

[53] Account joins Clarke's here.

[54] This section copied from Purchas, p. 381. Purchas himself got the information from Richard Whitbourne's 1620 printed account of his journey to Newfoundland. *A Discourse and Discovery of New Found Land* (London, 1620), p. 11 The extracts in both books are identical, so it is impossible to tell which was the one consulted by this author. Because

far distant, as England is from the nearest part of France, and lies between 46 and 53 degrees, North-Latitude. It is nearly as spacious as Ireland and lies near the course that ships usually hold on their return from the West Indies, and near half the way between Ireland and Virginia. The greatest part of the island lies above three degrees nearer to the South then any land of England does. The winter there is very mild, and the air temperate and wholesome, so that of the many [.....] upon the Coast, it is rare to see a sick person, and rarer that any dies. The natural inhabitants are few, savage, yet tractable[55] and in their habits, customs and manners, resemble the Indians of the continent from whom (it is supposed) they came, and live in the North and West part of the country. All along the coast of the country are many spacious and excellent bays, some of them stretching into the land, one towards another, more than 20 Leagues, and the bottoms of them meet together within the compass of a small circuit, by which means the passage over land from bay to bay is very facile and convenient. The Grand-Bay, where the whale-fishing is, lies on the North Side of the country, and round about the coast and in the bays, there are many small islands (none of them further off than a League from the land) both fair and fruitful, and no part of the world affords greater store of good harbours, more free from dangers, or more commodious than are there built by

---

other notes are taken from Purchas, we can assume that this is a common source for all notes.

[55] Purchas and Whitbourne refer to natives as 'rude and savage', and then later claim that 'the French and Biscaynes' call the natives 'tractable'. In omitting this, the commonplace author is perhaps trying to give the impression that his knowledge about Newfoundland does not come from 'foreign' sources.

the admirable workmanship of God, in some of which are arms of rivers, long and large enough for many hundred sail of ships, to moor fast at anchor near a mile from the harbour's mouth. There is a great plenty of Codfish round about the coast and in the bays, but in the North part most of any other do the English practise fishing; and in some years formerly there has been 250 sail of ship every year at one time a fishing there which usually catch 120000 fish every ship one with another which sold at several markets in England, France and Spain at the rate of four pounds for every 1000 fish. Sixscore to the 100 which is not a penny a fish, amounts to 22000 pounds.

[56]The Bank which is called the Great Bank is not far from New-found-land and are mountains grounded in the depth of the waters which are raised up to 30, 35 and 40 fathoms,[57] near to the surface[58] or upper face of the sea. This bank is held by mariners to be 200 Leagues in length and 18,20 and 24 Leagues broad, which being passed there is no more bottom found than in these parts, until one come to the land. Here is excellent fishing for cod also, which in great shoals frequent the bank of which the Green-fish is made and are so called being undried, for that they must go on land for

---

[56] This extract is taken from Purchas page 247 which in turn is derived from Marc Lescarbot's account *Nova Francia*, pp. 46-48, first published in 1609.

[57] Commonplace author spells this 'faddoms' which is closer to Lescarbot's rendering 'Faddoms' than Purchas's 'fathoms'.

[58] Commonplace author inserts 'surface' here in order to explain the unusual term 'upper face of the sea'.

drying of them.[59] When the ships come to it, they have warning by birds, which are well known and by the French called hastfoyes, that is, liver-catchers, because of their greediness to devour the livers of the cod-fishes that are cast into the sea. The ships being here arrived, the sails are furled up and there is the fishing made for the green fish; there are other banks further off, unto which many that know the places go to fish. In fishing they sometimes take sea-dogs, whose skins are by joiners of great esteem for smoothing their work; and the French who frequent the bank use much of the hearts, guts and other inward parts (most delicate) of the Cod-fish, which they mince, with lard and spices, and with those things make as good Bologna Sausages, as any can be made in Paris.[60]

7.[61] In the navigation on the western seas toward America and the parts adjacent such as New-found-land and other places on the coast, the mariners have found strange heat both in the sea itself and in the air; for in some voyages the sea water has been found very warm for three days and by the same warmth, wine and other beverages also were warm

---

[59] Here the commonplace author omits a section found both in Lescarbot and Purchas describing an attached map and also the seasickness of some of the French sailors. It seems that it is the navigation, flora and fauna that interest the author, not the experiences of individual explorers.

[60] Commonplace author omits 'and we did eat of them with a very good stomach'. Again, he is taking notes covering concrete information about the country and not about this particular voyage.

[61] Commonplace author starts a new paragraph but continues to copy from Purchas pp 246-7 and Lescabot, pp 46-48. Any first person narrative is removed and replaced with 'mariners find...'

in the bottom of the ship, yet the air is not hotter than before, that being then in the middle of June and but three days after quite contrary, being encompassed with such mists and colds as they thought themselves to be in the month of December, the water of the sea being also extreme cold, which continued till coming near New-found-land by reason of the said mists, which outwardly procured the cold. The reason of the Antiperistase is attributed to the ices of the North, which come floating down upon the coast and sea adjoining to Newfoundland and Terra de Labrador which is brought thither with the sea, by her natural motion, which is greater there than elsewhere because of the great space it hath to run, as in a Gulf, in the depth of America, where the nature and situation of the universal earth doth bear it easily. Now these ices (which sometimes are seen in banks of 10 Leagues length and as mountains are far deeper in the waters) holding as it were, an empire in the sea, drive out from them that which is contrary to their coldness, and consequently, do bind and close on the side that small quantity of mild temperature that the summer may bring to that part, where they come to seat and place themselves. And these cold mists and fogs may be perceived (a far off) to come and warn about a ship, holding the mariners prisoners 3 or 4 days, for one day of fair and clear weather they permit which are always accompanied with cold, by reason of the [...] absence; yes, diverse thick fogs have been seen to continue 7 or 8 days together without show of sun, or but very little and the reason of such effect is probably conceived to be this.

As the fire draws the moisture[62] of a wet cloth opposite unto it, so likewise the sun draws moisture and vapours, both from the sea and from the land, but for dissolving them, there is in these parts one virtue and beyond them another, according to the accidents and circumstances that are met with. In the European countries as France, England and so[63] on the sun raises up vapours only from the ground and from rivers, which earthly vapours, gross and weighty, and participating less of the moist element, do cause a hot air, and the earth discharged of those vapours, comes through more hot and parching; from thence it comes that the said vapours, having the earth on the one part and the sun on the other which heats them, they are easily dissolved, not remaining long in the air, unless it be in Winter, when the earth is grown cold and the sun far off, beyond the Equinoctial Line. From the same reason proceeds the cause why mists and fogs are not so frequent in the lesser seas,[64] as the New-found-land because there the sun, passing from his rising, above the grounds, this sea at the coming thereof, receives almost no other but earthly vapours, and by a long space retains the virtue to dissolve very soon, the exhalation it draws to itself; but when it comes to the midst of the ocean, and to the said New-found-land, having drawn up and assumed so long a course, a great abundance of vapours,

---

[62] Both Lescarbot and Purchas refer to 'moistness' whereas our commonplace author has changed this to 'moisture'.

[63] Lescarbot and Purchas refer to 'these our countries', so the commonplace author is English and is aware that he is reading an account by a Frenchman. By naming the countries he shows that the notes will be useful if revisited later.

[64] Lescarbot and Purchas refer to 'the French seas'.

from this most spacious ocean, it does not so easily dissolve them; as well because those vapours are cold of themselves, and of their own nature, as because the element which is nearest unto them doth sympathize with them and preserves them; and the sun beams being not helped and assisted in the dissolving of them, as they are upon the earth, which is seen in the land of that country which (although the heat be not great by reason of the abundance of Woods) not withstanding it helps to disperse the mists and thick fogs, (it being fair weather on land during the mists at sea) which be ordinarily there in the morning during Summer, but not as at sea for about 8 or 9 of the clock[65] in the morning, they begin to vanish away and serve as a dew to the ground.

[8][66] There is a certain strange[67] beast in New-England, which the natives call a moose, he is as big bodied as an ox, [....] like a fallow deer with a broad palm which he moves every year, as those do, but his neck is like a red deer [....] short mane, running along the ridge[68] of his back, his hair is shaggy[69] like an elk, he hath likewise a great wick[70] hanging

---

[65] Both Lescarbot and Purchas have written only '8 o'clock', this means that the author is actively considering what he is copying and amending sections that he deems to be inaccurate.

[66] Taken from Purchas, p. 352 in turn derived from *A Brief Relation concerning the discovery of New England* (1622), p. 14.

[67] Word 'strange' added by commonplace author.

[68] Purchas and anonymous author have word 'raines' of his back.

[69] Originals have word 'long': author trying to be more emotive and descriptive.

[70] Both Purchas and the anonymous author have 'bunch' instead of 'wick'.

down under his throat, and is of the colour of the blacker sort of fallow deer in old England. His legs are long, and his feet as big as the feet of a large ox, his tail is longer than the single of a deer, and reaches almost down to his huxens. His skin makes very good buff, and his flesh is excellent good meat. The natives make themselves jerkins of the skins of the beast, which they dress very well, keeping them all the year to serve their turn, and so prove very serviceable for their use. Many of them frequent a great island upon the coast called Mount Monsel by the English, whither the savages use to go at certain seasons to hunt them: the manner whereof is by making several fires and setting the country with people, drive them by force into the sea, to which indeed the beast is naturally addicted then there are others that when they are in the sea attend them in their boats with bows and arrows, and other weapons of several kinds, where with they kill and take as many as they please.[71]

[72]There is in Virginia a little beast of a strange incredible nature, called the Apossume, it is about the bigness of a pig

---

[71] It is intriguing that the commonplace author did not transcribe the next sentence which described the possibility of the usefulness of the moose as a draught animal. This was never successfully accomplished and perhaps this was common knowledge by the time he wrote or he did not believe it himself.

[72] Purchas page 287. His description of the possum is derived from John Smith's A *Map of Virginia* (1612) but neither quite replicate this version. The possum had fascinated readers such as Simon Forman from James I's reign. 'There is also a beast called a opossom', wrote Forman, 'and it is as bige as an old cat but a face like a rat and his head is also like a rat...and this beast doth carry her yonge ones in her belly and she hath under her belly a bag where she carrieth her yong ones up and down...they will goe out of that bag and feed and then goe into yt again and they live by grasse and hearbes and by ded fish on the sea side'. One

of 2 months old. She hath commonly 7 young ones at a time, sometimes more and sometimes fewer, and till the young ones be 5 months old, she at her pleasure can take them all up into her belly, and put them forth again without hurt to herself or them at all; the flesh of the beast is a very pleasant, wholesome, and nourishing food.[73]

[74]In Brazil, there are a kind of monkey, which the natives[75] call Sagouin, it is of a reddish coloured hair and no bigger than a squirrel; but as touching the shape, the snout, neck,

---

of the earliest printed mentions of the possum in an English book was in *A True Declaration of the State of Virginia*, a Virginia Company tract published in 1610. Possums are briefly mentioned alongside raccoons as being 'in shape like to pigges'. The similarities are striking between Forman's comments and a section in Strachey's 'Historie of Travell into Virginia Britannia', not written until after Forman's death according to some historians. Strachey compares the possum's size to 'a pretty beagle', rather than Forman's cat. However, Strachey may have suggested to Forman the idea that the female possum's pouch is like a bag: he writes 'she carryes her yong ones under her belly in a piece of her own skynn like as in a bagge'. The description of the pouch was not mentioned in *A True Declaration*. Forman also may have read a manuscript of John Smith's 'A Map of Virginia', not printed until after Forman's death, in 1612. It is Smith who described the possom as having 'a head like a swine, and a taile like a rat and about the bignes of a cat'.

[73] Interesting to compare Samuel Clarke's 1657 description of the curigue and the armadillo: the armadillo is as big as a pig and tastes 'pleasantly', and the curigue carry their young in a pouch and normally have 6 or 7 young. It seems as though the description of the possum found here is actually a combination of Clarke's description of two different animals.

[74] Taken from Purchas page 97 (in turn derived from account by Hans Staden).

[75] In the original, 'Americans'. By the time the commonplace author was writing this could refer to settlers of European descent, so he uses the word 'natives' to clarify.

breast, and almost all the other parts, being very like a lion; it is also hardy, and excels in beauty every little beast there. If it could be brought over sea it would be of great price and estimation; but the little body is so weak, that it cannot endure the working of a ship; for it is of that haughtiness of spirit, that if it be offended never so little, it will die through discontent. Another but far stranger beast this country affords called by the savages[76] Coaty; it is as big as a hare, with short and spotted hair, little and strange ears, a little head, with an eminent snout, from the eyes more than a foot long, and round as any cane, but suddenly decreasing at the end, so that it is all along of an equal thickness, with a mouth so little, as it cannot receive a man's little finger. When this wild beast is taken, she will gather her four feet together, and bend her self to the one side or the other, or fall flat down, nor can she ever be raised, or compelled to eat, unless ants be given her; on which she also feeds in the woods. A beast more monstrous than this is hardly to be found. A third beast as strangely deformed as this is that which the natives call Hay; it is of the bigness of a cur dog, with a belly hanging down like a sow ready to furrow, the hair of it is of an ash-colour that hath been washed, with a very long tail, hairy feet like a bear, and long sharp claws; while it is in the woods, it is very fierce, yet being taken is very easily tamed. The savages[77] do not love to play with them because they have both long and sharp claws. They say it lives only on air.

---

[76] In Purchas 'Barbarians'

[77] In Purchas 'Tupinamba'

9. There are several sorts of parrots in Brazil, in the continent of America, one whereof is a great and very fair parrot, which the Indians call Ajcurous. These are beautified with diverse fine coloured feathers, the head is intermingled with a scarlet red, a golden yellow, and violet colours, the ends of his wings crimson or rose-colour; the tail, which is very long is all yellow, and all the rest of the body green. They are as big as a cock pheasant.[78] One of this kind a Brazilian woman kept, which as if she had been endued with reason, conceived those things which she was commanded. This woman lived in a village near unto an island where there was a colony of Frenchmen[79] and as often as any of them went that way, the mistress of the bird would come out to them and say, if you will give me a comb, or a looking-glass, I will presently command my parrot to sing and dance before you and if her request was granted, the parrot presently upon hearing certain words uttered by her mistress did not only dance on the perch where she sat, but also prattled and whistled, and lastly most wonderfully counterfeited the savages going to the wars making such a hubbub as they then do,[80] that if her mistress thought good to bid her sing, she sung, if to dance, she danced, or if to whistle, she whistled. Whatsoever her mistress commanded her to do, she distinctly did. On the contrary, if they rewarded not the woman, she with a little sharper speech would command the bird, their Auge, that is, be still, then

---

[78] This sentence is not included in the original. Perhaps the colour of the birds reminded the commonplace author of a cock pheasant.

[79] This does not appear in Purchas: seems to be by way of explanation.

[80] In the original 'counterfeited the barbarians going to the wars'.

she presently held her peace, nor could any of them with any words make her to move either her tongue or feet, never so little. Now if the Romans had had such a parrot in Rome, they would have esteemed her as highly, as they did the raven, which as Pliny records it, Lib: 10, Ch: 43.[81] did every morning fly from his Masters, a shoemaker's shop to the top of the rostra, the public pulpit for orations, where turning to the forum and market place, she bid good morrow to the Emperor Tiberius, and after him to the young Princes Germanicus and Drusus, every of them by their names, and then to the people as they passed by, and this duty the bird did for many years, to all men's wonder in Rome: and being killed, by an envious neighbour, had the solemn rites of funeral, and he that killed this bird was punished with death.[82] The woman called her parrot Cherinbaue, that is, her best beloved: and indeed she was so dear to her, that being demanded what her price was, the woman in a scoffing manner answered, Mocaouasson, that is, a great brass gun, so that the parrot could not be wrested from her at any price.

10.[83] In the year of our Lord 1610 Captain Richard Whitburne being in St John's Harbour in New-found-land, and as he was in a morning early, standing by the water side he spied a strange creature very swiftly to come swimming

---

[81] This is a rare instance in which the commonplace author transcribes a Classical reference.

[82] This extract not included in Purchas, perhaps the commonplace author was familiar with Pliny.

[83] Taken from Purchas, p 382. Also very similar to Samuel Clarke, p. 56. Whitbourne, p. 46 Purchas's account most similar to this, and his was derived from Whitbourne's. This is nearly a word for word transcription.

towards him, looking cheerfully, as it had been a woman, by the face, forehead, eyes, nose, mouth, ears, chin and neck. It seemed to be beautiful, and in those parts so well proportioned having round about upon the head, blue streaks resembling hair down to the neck and which certainly was hair for the Captain says he beheld it a long time and another of his company also, that was not then far from him, and seeing the same coming so swiftly towards him, he gave back for it was come with the length of a pike, which when the strange creature saw and that he went from it, it presently thereupon dived a little under water and did swim to the place which before he landed, whereby he beheld the shoulders and back [...] it down to the middle, to be as square, white, and smooth as the back of any woman and from the [...] to the hinder part pointing in proportion like a broad headed arrow; how it was proportioned in the forepart he could not discern; but the same shortly after came unto a boat, wherein one William Hawkridge, the Captain's servant was with others, and the same creature did put both its hands upon the side of the boat ,and did strive to get into the boat to them whereat they were afraid, and she of them, struck it a full blow on the head, whereat it went away from them and afterwards it came to two other boats that were in the harbour, but the men in them made to the land [...] for fear. This creature then plunged itself into the water and was supposed to go to sea forthwith for it was seen no more neither then nor at any time after. It was thought by the Captain and the rest that plainly saw it to be a mermaid, this much the Captain related upon his own certain knowledge and sight a good while of the creature and because diverse had formerly written of mermaids, this strange creature seen by him in New-found-land he believed was a mermaid, yet whether this creature that himself and diverse of his company then saw was such a one he would not positive affirm, but left it for others to judge, by what he related.[84]

11.[85] There is a manner of hunting and hawking in the great ocean, representing that which men use on land, save only in the disposing of the game for by man's skill and industry, the hound and hawk is brought to that obedience, that whatsoever they seize is for their master but in the sea it is otherwise, for the game that is for him that seizes it. The dolphins and bonitos are the hounds and the alcatraces (or are some call them sparkites)[86] are the hawks, and the poor little flying fishes are the game.[87] The dolphin is one of the swiftest fishes in the sea; he is like a bream, but that he is longer and thinner and his scales very small; he is of the colour of the rainbow and his head different from other fishes: for from his mouth half a span it is freight upright, as the head of a wherry or the cut-water of a ship; there are some bigger, some lesser, but the greatest seldom above four foot long. The bonito is altogether like a mackerel, but that is somewhat more grown, and therefore is called the Spanish mackerel, there is another sort of them so great as one man

---

[84] Throughout this section, Whitbourne's first person description is rendered in the third person.

[85] Taken from Purchas p. 121 and similar to Clarke, p. 56.

[86] This is not in Purchas. Perhaps the commonplace author's personal knowledge is reflected here.

[87] Here the commonplaces author omits a section from Purchas that records that 'whose wonderfull making magnifieth the Creator'.

can hardly lift him. These from the fin of the tail forward have upon the chine seven small yellow hillocks, close to one another.[88] The Alcatrace is a sea fowl different from all either on the land or sea; his head is like that of a gull, and his bill like a woodcock's, and in all places alike. He is almost like a heronshaw, his legs a good span long, his wings are very long, and sharp towards the points, with a long tail like a pheasant, but with three or four feathers only, and those narrower. He is all black like a crow, of little flesh, but all skin and bones; he soars the highest of any fowl, and none has ever seen any of them rest in the sea. The flying fishes are in their making so wonderful, as magnifies the Creator, who for their safety has given them extraordinary manner of fins, which serve in stead of wings, like those of a bat of such a delicate skin, interlaced with bones so curiously, as may well cause admiration in the beholders. They are like pilchards in colour and making; saving that they are somewhat rounder, and for the most part bigger. They fly best with a side wind but longer than their wings be wet, they cannot sustain the weight of their bodies; so the greatest flight they can make is never above a quarter of a mile. They commonly swim in shoals and serve for food for the greater fishes and for the fowls. The dolphins and the bonitos do continually hunt after them, and the alcatraces lie soaring in the air to see when they spring out of the water or take their flight; and ordinarily he that escapes the mouth of the dolphin or the bonito helping himself by his wings, falls prisoner into the hands of the alcatrace, and helps to fill his gorge.

---

[88] The previous three sentences do not appear in Purchas or Clarke.

[12]. There are fishes that are perpetual enemies to the whale, the sword fish, and the thresher, who at once commences a war against this great Leviathan.[89] The swordfish is not great, but yet strongly made, and in the top of its line (as one may say) between the neck and the shoulders he has the form of a sword in substance unlike unto a bone firm and hard, three foot long and four or five inches broad, full of sharp prickles on either side along the edges; it is but thin, the greatest being the most commonly not above a finger thick. The thresher is a greater fish, whose tail is very broad thick and very weighty, and this is his weapon, where with he assaults the whale. They fight in this manner; the swordfish places himself under the belly of the whale, and the thresher upon the rise of the water. Then with his ponderous[90] tail he threshes the head of the whale very forcibly, till he forces him to give way, and to sink down deeper into the sea, to avoid the weight of those blows; which the swordfish perceiving, receiving him upon his sword and wounds him in the belly which is but tender, and so forces him to mount up again. (Beside that he cannot abide long under water, but must of force rise up to breathe) where the thresher assaults him with more blows; and when in this manner they torment him with a continued succession of blows and wounds some of the blows have in that fight been heard by mariners two Leagues off, as if it had been the

---

[89] This clause not included in Purchas or Clarke. The commonplace author may have included this as a Biblical reference (although he does not do this elsewhere) or he may have been familiar with Hobbes's *Leviathan*, published in 1651.

[90] 'Ponderous' is not in the original

report of a great piece of ordinance, the roaring of the whale being heard much further. It also happens sundry times, that in a great part of the surfaces of the sea, round about the place where this fight is, changes the colour with the blood of the wounded whale; which being in the extremity, has no way left to relieve himself, but to make with what speed he can to the next shore, which at the first sight of his adversaries he labours to procure, and that before the fight, for getting the shore, there can only one of his adversaries fight with him, and for either of them hand to hand, he is too good.

13.[91] Pedro Fernandez de Quiros, a Portuguese, a famous Pilot, was sent with two ships from Lima, the capital city of Peru anno 1609 to discover the islands of Solomon, which lie in the height of the Straits of Magellan. He discovered a main land, and sailed 800 Leagues upon the coast until he came to the height of 15 degrees, to the Southward of the Equinoctial Line. Touching the extent of which discovered country, called Terra Australis Incognita, reputed the fourth part of the world; the length thereof is said to be as great as all Europe and Asia the Less, unto the Sea of Bachu, Persia and all the islands, as well of the ocean as Mediterranean Sea, taking England and Ireland into the account. This country is the fourth part of the terrestrial globe, and extends itself to such length, that in probability it is much greater in kingdoms and seignories than all those which at the time did acknowledge subjection and obedience to the King of Spain and that without the neighbourhood, either of Turk or

---

[91] Taken from Purchas page 144.

Moors, or of any other Nation, which attempts war upon confining countries. This land is all seated within the Torrid Zone, and a great tract thereof reaches to the Equinoctial Circle. The breadth may be of 90 Degrees, and in some places a little less: and the people will doubtless upon a full discovery prove the Antipodes to the better part of Africa unto all Europe, and the greater portion of Asia; but it must be observed that as the countries already then discovered in 15 degrees of Latitude are better than Spain so that other which are opposite to that Elevation, must by proportion and analogy be a Terrestrial Paradise. There is in the coast a fair bay, of 20 Leagues into which there falls 2 great rivers out of the country, a place very proper for a plantation. There are also many islands in the same coast, both great and little, all very plentiful, and well inhabited.[92]

All those quarters swarm with an incredible multitude of inhabitants, whereof some are white, others black and in colour like Mulattos, or half Moors, and others of a mingled complexion; Some wear their hair long others crisp and both black, others have yellow locks which diversity is an apparent argument that there is commerce among them. They have no knowledge of artillery, no mines, no artificial trades, no forts nor walls, and live without the awe of King or laws. They are a simple people, cartoned into tribes. Their weapons are clubs, truncheons, pikes, bows and arrows. They are a tractable and neat people, and very modest and

---

[92] The last two sentences do not appear in Purchas. Suggests that the commonplace author may have had access to another source or had become confused in his reading (the sentences do not appear to follow on). It is not clear why this extract is in brackets in the original manuscript.

bashful, there is plenty of all sorts of timber, and fruit trees, fowl tame and wild, fish in abundance, in the sea and in the rivers, plants and gardening: Milk and Honey, and whatsoever else is necessary for man's sustenance. But the riches in those parts are gold, silver and pearl, the three most precious darlings that lie in the bosom of nature, and many sorts of spiceries and aromatical drugs, those countries lying very near the Parallel of Terinate Bachu, and the Moluccos.[93] The soil is fat, fertile and easily manurable; it affords clay for to make bricks and tiles for houses of necessary use, and marbles for structures of state and magnificence. There is a goodly haven called Porto de La Vera Cruz, of that spacious capacity, that it is able to contain 1000 ships. This haven and the bay is neighboured of many goodly islands, especially of 7 which are said to have 200 Leagues of extent and one of them (which is 12Leagues distant from the haven) is fifty Leagues in circuit, all very plentiful and well inhabited.[94]

This is in brief a description of the greatness and goodness of those Countries of which the said Pedro Fernandez de Quiros, took possession in the name of his Majesty of Spain, Don Philipe III after this manner. First he erected a cross, and thereby built a little Church in honour of our Lady of Loreto, then he caused 20 Masses to be celebrated and the

---

[93] This sentence strays away from Purchas's version considerably. He only mentions mother of pearl and does not mention gold, silver or spices or drugs.

[94] This last sentence does not appear in Purchas. Commonplace author regularly adds his own contextual geographical information.

feast of the blessed sacrament to be observed,[95] which was carried in solemn procession, the King's Banner[96] displayed, and marching before the said Sacrament through a great circuit of ground, which was honoured with the same. In three several places he set up the King's title at large in every of which was prepared and erected 2 columns the same with the arms of his Majesty tricked thereon, as an accomplishment of the Impress of Plus Ultra, because it stretched into the Continent, much enlarging the spaciousness of the Spanish Dominions, and adding to the titles which his Majesty already possesses, that of De La Australia Spiritu Santa, containing the fourth part of the world; which interest and title the Discoverer thus blazoned in the face of the world to the glory of God primarily who revealed this noble country; next to the honour of his Majesty the King of Spain, the rightful possessor thereof.[97]

14.[98] In a small island in the Straits of Magellan are great store of a certain fowl called penguins, and therefore called the islands of penguins. This penguin is a fowl in all proportion like a goose, and has no feathers, but a certain

---

[95] In Purchas's account, indulgences are mentioned here. It is obvious that Catholic practises are being described. This omission is odd considering the later focus of the commonplace book on Catholic religious ritual.

[96] In the original this is listed as 'your banner' as the text is derived from a manuscript letter to the king of Spain.

[97] The commonplace author omits part of the letter which concludes with the author 'prostrating himself' before his king.

[98] Taken from Purchas p. 125, who in turn took the extract word for word from Hawkins, p. 40.

down upon all parts of her body, and therefore cannot fly, but helps her self on all occasions with her feet, running as fast as a man. She lives in the sea and there feeds on fish, and on the Shore eats grass like a goose. They harbour themselves under ground in burrows as conies do, and in them hatch their young. All parts of the island where they haunt are undermined save only one valley, which (it seems) they preserve for their food, for it is at the Spring of the flourishing a green as the finest meadow. Their flesh tastes like that of a puffin[99] by which it is easily discerned that their chief food is fish. They are very fat and must be flayed like a bittern before dressing, and are reasonable meat roasted, baked or boiled,[100] but best roasted.[101] The mariners hunt them, kill them, split them then wash them well in sea-water then salt them in which they lie 6 hours, and in press 8 hours till the blood be soaked out, then salt them anew and put them into casks as is the custom to salt beef; being in this manner prepared they will continue good some 2 months, and serves them instead of beef.

Another part of the same island is inhabited only with ducks, different from those in England, and less good meat, yet in case of necessity will serve. There are abundance of them and as it were by consent possess a part of the island to themselves, which is the highest hill, and more than a

---

[99] In Purchas puffins are described as 'taken in Lundy and Scilly'.

[100] In Purchas 'sodden'.

[101] Here the commonplace author omits a section describing a bloody hunting trip that Hawkins himself called a 'massacre' in which a number of penguins were killed and eaten.

musket shot over: in creatures void of reason, there is none to be seen that shows greater art and curiosity in pacing and making their nests than they do; all the hill is so full of them that the exactest mathematician[102] that is could not devise how to place one more than there was upon the hill, one path only being left by them as a foot-path for a fowl to pass betwixt. The hill is all level, as if it had been[103] smoothed by Art. The nests are made only of earth, and seeming to be of the self same mould, for the nests and the soil are all one, which with water, that they bring in their bills they make into a clay, or a certain daub and after fashion them as exactly round as if done with a compass, in the bottom they contain the measure of a foot, the height is about 8 inches, and at the top is the same quantity over; there they are hollowed in somewhat deep wherein they lay their eggs without other presentation: and it is conceived that the sun helps them to hatch their young: their nests last for many years and are all of one proportion, not one exceeding another in bigness nor height and in a precise and proportionable distance one from another. In all this hill, nor in any of their nests was to be found a blade of grass, a feather, a straw, a stick, a moat, no, nor the muting or fitting of any fowl; but all the nests and spaces betwixt them so smooth, so neat and cleanly as if they had been newly swept and washed.

---

[102] In Purchas 'the greatest mathematician of the world'.

[103] Here and throughout Purchas writes 'beene' or 'been' but the commonplace author 'bin'. This occurs throughout and may be a sign of a particular dialect.

15.[104] In the year 1542, Francis Landre, Vicar of St Cross in Paris, taught the people sincerely and said no mass because he drank no wine, but whether he did so out of an antipathy in nature to wine or of set purpose, was not known;[105] against whom the doctors of Sorbonne had conceived a great hatred, having noted something in the preachings and so propounded unto him these Articles: that the sacrifice of the Mass was instituted by Christ, and is available[106] for the quick and the dead. That we must pray to saints that they may be Mei[....] | [....] be unto Christ; that the substance of bread and wine is changed in the Consecration. That only Priests may consecrate bread and wine and that the whole supper of the Lord appertains to them only.[107] That monastical vows must be kept: that by the sacraments of confirmation and unction, the Holy Ghost is received. That by prayer, fasting and good works souls are delivered out of purgatory. That the Laws of the Church concerning fasting and choice of meats, so bind the conscience that there is one High Prelate and Bishop of the Church whom all are bound to obey, by the Law of God. That many things must be

---

[104] Taken from Johannes Sleidanus, *A Famous Cronicle of Our Time called Sleidanes Commentaries,* trans. John Day (London, 1560) p 198. This section reveals a very different area of interest from the focus on travel in the first 14 paragraphs. This single book provides the source material for paragraphs 15-35.

[105] In the original 'I know not'. Commonplace author removing reference to first person.

[106] In later versions of Sleidanus' *Chronicles*, the word 'propitiatory' appears here: 'available' has a different meaning, conveying none of the idea of atoning.

[107] This shows the Protestant influence on Sleidanus in calling the sacrament 'the Lord's Supper'.

believed and of necessity received, that are not expressed in the Scriptures. That the pardons[108] of the Bishop of Rome do release the pains of purgatory. That Priests being never so sinful and vicious, do consecrate the Lord's body. That all deadly sin must be confessed to the Priest, and then to receive Sacramental Absolution of him. That man has free charity and true penance is obtained remission of sins. That the Church and a General Council being lawfully assembled can not err, and therefore must be obeyed. That the judgment and interpretation of the Scripture appertains to the Church if anything be in controversy; all of which things they would have had him subscribe to and to confirm with his seal. But he after 2 days consideration, answered in general terms, that whatsoever the Holy Catholic Church has taught in these matter, is good and godly; but they not content with this doubtful answer, proceeded further against him not long after seeing him to persevere still in his Preaching, where upon by the procurement of these divines which had accused him to the Lieutenant Criminal, he was committed to prison.

Within a few days after his Commitment, King Francis[109] came to Sangermane, which is a little Town with a castle near the River of Seine, 5 Miles beneath Paris,[110] and being

---

[108] In later editions written as 'indulgences'. This shows that Sleidanus's rhetoric is less forcefully Protestant than in later editions.

[109] Commonplace author includes the words 'King Francis' for explanatory purposes; it is rendered only as 'the king' in the original.

[110] Location explained by commonplace author, not in the original. There follows in the original a similar example of a preacher called Depensius,

informed of the whole matter called the preacher before him; He when he came thither being put in fear by some that told him, that he was in danger of his life for that the King was greatly offended with him, began to relent and recede from his former constancy of Spirit, which many did not look for at his hands; and being carried again to Paris, he was enforced to recant all such things as he had taught before. For in the Cathedral Church April 29th 1543 did assemble the Senators and Judges of the Parliament, all the Magistrates and Officers of Paris, and a great number of Divines. After the Church doors were made fast and soldiers in their arms to guard the same, to keep out the people. When all were placed, his opinions were openly read, and being demanded of every one what he believed there in, he answered, as pleased them and withal confessing and declaring that he had erred, and promised all humble obedience from thenceforth, and further did acknowledge those above-mentioned Articles of Doctrine, which first the Divines, and after the King's Counsel propounded to him to be true and godly; to the which when he had sealed and subscribed, and withal all openly declared that this his recantation was free, voluntary, and unenforced, he was with gentle admonitions, dismissed.[111]

---

ignored by our commonplace author because it illustrates the same point as the Landre case.

[111] The last clause not found in the original, included to explain what had happened to Landre, but taken from an unknown source.

16.[112] In the time of King Francis I of France lived Clement Marot who, in the vulgar tongue, far surmounted all the Poets, that either were before his days or that lived also in his time in France. Tis true, he had no greater skill in nor knowledge of the Latin tongue: but yet could with such as were learned therein, he posited very much therein; neither was there any thing almost in the books of the poets that writ in Latin, but he knew it; [...] that out of their works he took much, and applied it to his purpose. Thus did he covertly translate things out [...] Tibellus, Horace, Propertius, Virgil, Ovid, Persius and Martial, into his works, and out of Catullus he took the marriage of Hercules, Duke of Ferrara, and Renate, daughter to Lewis 12, King of France. He translated also most excellently, the first Book of Ovid's Metamorphoses. And in his latter days, bent all his ingenuity to compose Divine Poems, taking his subject matter out of the Holy Scriptures, and intended to turn all the Psalms of David into French metre. But he was surprised with sickness whereof he died before he had fully finished 50 Psalms, which now remain and are read not without the admiration of his transcendent wit; for nothing is more pleasant than his style, nothing purer than his speech, nothing sweeter or apter than the cadence of his rhythms. And what he had writ he published in print at Geneva, anno 1543[113] whither he repaired some time before, because he might not with safety make his abode any longer in France upon suspicion of being inclined to Lutheranism. He had printed 30 Psalms 2 years before in Paris, but with much difficulty because no

---

[112] Sleidanus, p. 207.

[113] 'this year' in the original.

book was to be printed there before the Doctors of Sorbonne had perused the same and licensed it for the press, with an Imprimatur under the hand of some of that faculty, that nothing was contained there in contrary to sound Doctrine, and the Christian faith. The memory of this excellent person is still recent in France and his name (where the language he writ in is understood) is celebrated in other nations and shall endure to all posterity. And most men of judgement are of opinion that it is hard for any man to match him in this way of writing poems, and of him it may be said, what Tully[114] reported of Julius Caesar, that he made all wise men afraid to write; some others have taken in hand the same argument, and indeed better learned than he, but none of them could ever yet attain to that elegancy of style, and perfect finesse of expression which he writ in.

17.[115] When the French king Francis I[116] had set forth severe edicts[117] against the Lutherans, anno 1542, the Parliament of Paris charged the printers there under a great penalty, not to print or publish any books condemned or suspected of heresy, and in particular Calvin's Institutions and also at the request of the Inquisitor, the King made a Decree that the Preachers should admonish the people to do their duty to the Church and if they knew any Lutheran or one that thought amiss in religion to present him, for that such a work was

---

[114] 'Cicero' in later versions of the original.

[115] Sleidanus, p. 198.

[116] In the original 'during this war, the king...'

[117] In the original 'proclamations': severe added to give the impression of Pope's intractable nature.

most acceptable to God; and the parish priests had an order prescribed them, which they were to follow in that enquiry. For they were to enquire of any that could inform them, whether they knew any man that should say that there was no purgatory; that when a man is dead to be either saved or damned; that God only must be called upon, and not saints, that a man is not justified by observing God's Commandments; that the worshipping of images is idolatry; that saints work not miracles; that the ceremonies of the Church profit nothing; that the laws of the church do bind no man; that the knowledge of the Gospel is necessary for all men, without exception; that it is a fond part[118] for the common people to pray to God in [....] that the Priest cannot forgive sins, through the sacrament of Penance, but to be only a Minister, to pronounce the benefit of God, who forgives our sins; that the Church can bind no man to mortal sin; that it is lawful to eat flesh at all times.

This form of Inquisition was given privately to priests but besides this a proclamation was openly set forth, wherein they were commanded to be presented and punished, which neglected the laws of the Church or such as had books contrary to the Christian faith and either give themselves to read, or purposely drop them in the way they go, that they may be found. Those that assemble in private gardens and houses and forge devises against the laws of the Church and they that receive such kind of men into their houses or gardens, they that are privy to any such thing are commanded to present them within 6 days to the Doctors of Divinity chosen by the Inquisitor, or else to stand accused.

---

[118] In later versions of the original 'an idle thing'.

Lastly, the Stationers were also charged, that if they had anything either printed or written that was in any point suspected or that swayed from the custom of the Church that within 6 days they should bring before them for after, no excuse would serve.[119] The same day that this was proclaimed, there was a general procession ordered for preservation of religion and the realm, and St Genevese, a Swiss, the trusty saint which in Paris is worshipped above all other saints whose image is ever carried with great pomp in all dangers, when God's wrath is to be appeased, the Church's peace disturbed or war or famine feared: in such cases the Parisians fly unto her, as to the Anchora Spei,[120] and in port of their succour; the people are persuaded, that her help was never yet delivered in pain; insomuch that some do blasphemously[121] say, that God can do very much, but St Genevese is the saviour of Paris in such processions, this image (by an old custom) is carried by 4 butchers, which prepare themselves hereunto certain days before, by fasting and prayer and when it is carried about, the people run unto it on every side, with great devotion, and happy are they that can but touch it with a fingers end, or with a cap or handkerchief: which makes the throng and press of people so great[122] that there are officers appointed to make way for

---

[119] From here to the end of the paragraph does not appear in the 1670 edition of Sleidanus, but it is in the original 1560 version, pp. 26-27. Thus, conclusively, the commonplace author was working with the earlier version.

[120] In the original 'last anker and port of their succour'.

[121] 'blasphemously' inserted.

[122] In the original 'beyond all reason'.

the procession and image, which is not done without much pain and trouble.

18.[123] John Calvin, anno 1543 writ a book in French of the Relics of Saints, which the Romanists superstitiously reverence, and profanely adore, to the intent that the age he himself lived in, and also that the age to come might see into what a sad case religion was brought. But what he mentions of these things, is only of such as were known to him, and wishes that the same were done likewise in other places and countries. Of this number together in his book, are the crib, or manger, wherein our saviour was laid at his birth, the swaddling cloths, a bearing cloth, the foreskin and blood, shed at his circumcision, partly pure and partly allayed with water, the water-pots of stone, that were at the marriage in the city of Cana in Galilee, the wine that Christ made then the Water they were filled with, the stuff and furniture of the chamber wherein he with his disciples eat his Maundy or Last Supper, the cross, the cane, the nails, sponge, lance, Crown of Thorns, the seamless coat, shoes, handkerchief, sweat in the garden, and tears of Christ, the hair, milk, smock, girdle, slippers, petticoat, comb, and ring of the Virgin Mary, the manna the people of Israel were fed with in the wilderness, the sword and buckler of Michael the Archangel, the feathers of a wing of the angel Gabriel, the skull, the jawbone, brains, and a finger of St John the Baptist, the chair, honlet, and massing garments and brains of St Peter. And then the bodies of saints and the same in diverse and sundry places. He then shows in his book with

---

[123] Sleidanus, pp. 210-211.

what veneration the people worship these things, which yet the priests will not without money so much as let them have sight off, though at a distance in themselves mere trifles and things of nought, which if they be well considered, appear to be nothing but craft and considered by the cunning priests for lucre. But now in Germany (he said) there be 2 famous cities stored with these commodities, viz. Therere, and Acon, for thither they say, devout people, men and women were wont to repair, as far as Slovenia and Hungary, to see and worship the precious and holy relics that were there. The [...] | that those merchants[124] exposed their wares, who but every 7th year that the admiration and estimation of them might be the greater, when they were so rarely seen.

19.[125] When the gladsome news was with a wonderful expedition brought to Rome of the reduction of England the Roman Church, in Queen Mary's: time, anno 1555, there was great joy in the whole city, and Te Deum was sung in every Church. After on Christmas Eve, the Pope sent abroad this Indulgence for so happy a condition. Since I heard England which of many years was rent and separated from the body of the Church is through the unmeasurable mes[sage] of God brought to me by the Communion of the same Church and to the obedience of the See of Rome, by the singular diligence, travail, fidelity and industry of the most precious King Philip and Queen Mary his Wife, and

---

[124] Hucksters in the 1670 original. Marchants in the 1560 original. The later version puts an even stronger anti-Catholic spin on events depicted.

[125] Sleidanus (1560), p. 450.

his eminence[126] Car[dinal] Pole, I took great pleasure in my mind; and also (as reason was) gave thanks unto god as heartily as [I] could, and omitted nothing but that the fruit of this my gladness might redound to this whole city. But as like [...] father, mentioned in the holy Gospel, having recovered his lost Son, not only rejoices exceedingly is privately glad in his mind, but also invited others to feast and make good cheer with him; even so I verily to intent that all the world may understand, how great my joy and gladness is, will that common thanks and prayers be ma[de]. Therefore, by the power that I have, I permit every man in general, that he may choose him, a priest whom he [...] unto whom he may confess his sins rightly, and do hereby give authority to the same priest that he may forgive all manner of sins, be they never so heinous even those which are reserved to my own power alone and are wont to be excepted by name; that he may remit not only the trespass, but also the pains for sins due; that he may impose such penance and satisfaction as behoves, and may release all vows except chastity and religion, yet so that they may be recompensed by another work. Yea trusting unto God's mercy, and the intercession of Sts Peter and Paul, I grant full remission of all sins, which is wont only to be given, but every 50 year, to all those that with an humble heart to turn to God and wholly confess all their sins. When they shall understand the Indulgence to be set forth by us twice or thrice a week, fast, and give alms, and use other god [...] and after receive the sacrament with thankfulness and

---

[126] 'his eminence' not included in original. This is unusual, as though the Catholic Pole is being given his fully honorary title by the commonplace author.

prayers to God, that he with the Light of his [...] [...] humble those that [...] darkness, there he would give peace, and move the hearts

[127]eth on the water, and when it is finished, he goes thrice about it and first besprinkles the upper walls, then the middle and after then the lowest of all, but still with this holy water. Then the Bishop with his crosier staff makes the Sign of the Cross, upon the highest walls that the Devil that foul fiend do not approach. After that he goes in to the Church whilst there is music and singing of anthems therein which end,[128] a Priest comes with a basin full of ashes, which he strews on the pavement in the form of a cross, the breadth of a palm of a man's hand; which done, the Bishop with his crosier writes Greek letters in the said ashes, at the left side of the cross, and Latin letters on the right, and last of all has another water brought him, which is a mixture of wine and ashes with some salt where with he all to besprinkled the Church: over again, and then makes an exhortation to the people which tends chiefly to stir them up to bountifulness and liberality for the Church's maintenance so with his blessing dismisses them, and departs.

[129]The hallowing of an altar by the Papists[130] is thus; first comes the Bishop into the Church: where the altar is erected attended by the priests and other officers thereunto

---

[127] Although this starts in the middle of a word, it does not follow on from the previous page indicating that a manuscript page is missing. This section is taken from Sleidanus, p. 340.

[128] Original 'when certain songs are ended'.

[129] Sleidanus, pp. 340-341.

[130] 'by the papists' is added, in the original 'they' is used.

belonging; and being seated in a chair, provided on purpose, then they bring oil, chrism, salt, wine, water, ashes, hyssop, a pound of frankincense, and a pan with hot coals, one coarse cloth to wipe with and another finer and softer to cover with, 5 crosses of wax, a chalice, a mortar, and 2 tapers and whatsoever else […] pertains to the furniture of an altar. And whilst these things are a bringing and ordering, the Bishop rises up and with the priests say certain prayers, and repeat some psalms. Then doth he besprinkle the altar with holy water in 5 several places but so disposing and bestowing the said water, that it doth represent the sign of the cross. He then goes 7 times about the altar and ends thereon another water temper with wine, ashes and hyssop. Moreover he mixes clay and water together and pours it upon the ground about the altar. Then the relics of saints are solemnly brought forth and laid upon the altar, which after they be censed, are again laid up in their due place. After this the Bishop swings the altar thrice about with the censors, which he then delivers to the priest who censes continually, till the hallowing be quite finished. Then the Bishop draws out 3 crosses of oil in several places upon the altar, and then pours out the oil and supples it in, and taking five small pieces of frankincense, and as many crosses made of wax, he places them here and there on the altar and after sets them on fire, the ashes whereof are gathered and kept as holy. Last of all, he anoints the 4 corners, the edges all along, and the forefront of the altar, and says[131] Mass. It is to be noted; that the chrism as they call it, and the oil is

---

[131] 'singeth' in the original. Perhaps this is significant, not wishing to associate singing in church with Catholicism.

consecrated in all places only on Maundy Thursday in the passion week, next before Easter.

The Papists have also a form of Hallowing of Bells, which is accustomed to be done in this manner: first the bell must hang so as the Bishop must go round it, then he repeats certain Psalms, after which salt and water is brought to him, which he consecrates severally, and then mingles them together, where with he washes the bell diligently both within and without, and when it is wiped very dry, the sign of the cross[132] is drawn on it, which consecrated last, and the Bishop prays unto God, that when the bell shall be rung or sounded, the Devil and all his craft and temptations[133] [...] vanish away; and that lightening and thunder, hail, winds and tempests[134] may be assuaged; and then he wipes out the cross of oil with a linen cloth and makes 7 other crosses on the outside of the bell and one only within and then repeating other Psalms, he takes a pair of censors and censes the bell within, and keeling down, he prays God, to send it good luck. In many places it is a custom to have a great dinner, and to keep a feast as if it were a solemn wedding.

[135]Before the Reformation which was wrought about 140 years ago, these and many other Popish ceremonies were had in great estimation and reverence with all men. But when Martin Luther, and after him other ministers of the

---

[132] In the original 'with holy oyle'. This omission seems merely an error of copying.

[133] In the original 'deceits'

[134] In the original 'intemperate weathers'

[135] In the original, 'in times past' is used instead of giving a number of years since the Reformation.

Gospel taught how that all creatures were consecrated by the mouth of God himself, at the time he created the whole world, all this gear came into contempt and mockery, as full of trumpery and juggling. And as for the consecration and antiquity of their holy water as they term it, there is a decree in the Pope's Decretals,[136] which are his law, which they ascribe to Alexander the fifth Bishop after S[t] Peter, who sat in the chair only 10 months and 5 days, anno 121[137] to the extent the thing may be of more credit and authority, by reason of the antiquity thereof.

24. [138] When a General Council is called, the which for some late ages the Pope hath assumed the safe authority to summon, the same is commonly so summoned, in case of some upstart He [....] opinion tending to the disturbance of the Church's peace, by causing schisms and divisions therein and in such cases his Holiness pretends to be the sole judge, but for the manner of supposing any heresy, he is willing to leave to such a Council as he doth call and is awed with the presence of his Legate, who presides therein, and other Divines and Prelates his creatures, nor are the parties accused of any Heretical opinion permitted to be present to speak for themselves when as all ecumenical councils ought to be free, and no person excluded, that have ought to say in

---

[136] This is added, in the original 'in the bishop of Rome's law'.

[137] Detail of Alexander's term of office not included in Sleidanus.

[138] Sleidanus, pp. 373-4. This section, paragraph 24, is unusual in that it is not a word for word copy of the original but a summary of it. A large section in the original on the procedures of the Council of Trent and its make-up is omitted, with the focus instead on the discussion of Protestant writings in the Protestants' absence.

their own defence, and fully to be heard at least. Such was the practise of the late Council (so called) of Trent, which may more rightly be styled a Conventicle only because Luther and his party were not permitted to be there; against whom and the error by them promulgated as the Romanists termed them against the Christian faith and doctrine was that Conventicle called in which when an article of faith was to be made in confutation of Luther's Doctrine, that were certain themes or Doctrinal Theses's brought to the Divines with these self same words; that they should search and try whether they were heretical, and meet to be condemned by the Holy Synod; which themes they had collected out of the writings of Luther, Zwinglius, Bucer and such others. The divines were only assistants to the fathers, the Doctors of Divinity having no vote in passing Decrees and used daily to assemble in the Legate's house, and there for many hours to debate among themselves the said themes without interruption, that so as they submitted all they said to the judgement of the Church of Rome. And though no Protestant nor any of their factions or favourites were permitted to be present at any of these debates among the divines yet was the place indifferently for all others and the Popes, Legates and the residue of the fathers were many times present, and sat there as hearers only for the divines only spoke, and the opinions of every of them respectively were registered by the scribes as they spoke in order to every point; and when all had done reasoning when in debate any one erred in the faith, was accustomed to take up a month's space. The fathers then depart before to the Pope's Legate and before him exar [...] the opinions [....] divines, which the scribes had registered; after that a certain number of them chosen, which pushing all their opinions reduce a doctrine out of them and what thing should be determinate and believed in every point for an article of faith.[139] After that they condemn the contrary doctrine and errors as they call them, with a grievous censure, that not with so many words; all which things are related to the whole assembly and when they be thoroughly agreed, the matter comes into open session, as is aforesaid, and the decrees openly read. That done, the holy fathers[140] are demanded whether they allow the same. They answer all, that they please them well. So it is that the divines in the Council declare only what their opinion is of every matter; but the fathers and with them a few other mitred prelates have authority to determine. That thing which is thus decreed, they command to be sacred and holy, and call those decrees 'Canons'. These things were thus done indeed with all the circumstances of formality outward but those that were better acquainted with the intrigues of the court of Rome[141] will affirm that all those Articles of Faith and Doctrine were concluded on in a private junto[142] at Rome, in the Pope's presence and by his express command, and sent to his Legate in the Trent Conventicle in time that the divines in their reasonings and debates might follow that prescription and order so sent; many of the divines and some of the Bishops also having their dependencies and were then

---

[139] The phrase 'article of faith' is not in the original.

[140] 'bishops' in the original. An unusual change as 'Holy Fathers' sounds more Catholic.

[141] Original 'Romish matters'

[142] Here and below, the idea of a 'junto' belongs to the commonplace author, not the original.

maintained by him; therefore those that could do more than barely guess at the clandestine results and orders of this junto, which were daily posted away to Trent, started this sarcastic phrase,[143] that the Holy Ghost came many times from Rome to Trent in a cloak-bag, and well they might, because that the Pope sent oftentimes large packets and other dispatches in post, signifying to his Legates there what he would have done.

25.[144] Francis the King of France when he had reigned 32 years, died at Rambovillet, a day's journey from Paris, March 31 1547 to whom his son Henry II about 28 years of age succeeded; who immediately sent for Annes de Momorancy Constable of France and restored him to his former dignities, and had him in great estimation, having been out of favour for 6 years before, and lived a private life and such as were in greatest authority before were partly turned out of favour, partly displaced, and imprisoned, but especially she who had been his father's darling, Madam de Estampes.[145] This King's death was a great loss to the virtuous[146] of those times, for he loved learning and none was more liberal than he to advance the same; and through long use and custom, himself had attained much knowledge, never dining nor supping without serious discoursing with

---

[143] In the original 'a fond proverb'.

[144] Sleidanus, pp. 288-289.

[145] Original lists others in the same position: 'Those were the Cardinall of Tournon, Anebalde the Admiral, Grinian, the gouernour of the Frenche prouince, the Duke of Longeuale, Bayarde, Poline.'

[146] 'Students and learned men' in the original.

learned men such was James Coline and Peter Castellan, of whom he learned whatsoever was excellent in History, Geography, and the Mathematics, and the Poets,[147] and had also a perfect knowledge of all that the Secretaries of Nature had writ of beasts, birds, serpents, plants, herbs, metals and precious stone; but above all delighted in dissertations of scripture, having always about him, such as were the most scientific men of each profession and those besides that any art knowing had the freedom to infer arguments and disputes, which freedom made men studious, that in reasoning before him they might deserve the approbation and commendation of so noble and learned a prince. In his own tongue he was both eloquent and grave and to improve himself in the knowledge of the Oriental tongue, he employed such as were learned therein, to buy or copy out many both manuscripts and books in those languages,[148] so that he had a famous library, full of rare books, the keeper whereof was Chastellan.

On ye 24th of May following this learned and prince Maecenas[149] was interred in the Church of St Dennis in the place consecrated for the burial of the King of France and with his 2 sons, that died some years before, and till then were unburied. And while the funeral pomp was preparing for the deceased King his effigies was exquisitely made in wax, apparelled in rich robes, and exposed upon a bed of

---

[147] In the original 'poets, historiographers and cosmographers'.

[148] No mention in the original of 'oriental' languages, simply that he had people source 'old books' from 'Greece and Rome' for him.

[149] This is inserted by commonplace author, no mention of Maecenas in the original, perhaps showing that the commonplace author has had a classical education.

state for many days, his Crown, Sceptre and other regalia was laid on the bed by him, and at the usual hours both of dinner and supper he was served with the like state and solemnity as was accustomed being alive. After this, these robes of state were taken away and mourning apparel put on. There were 48 friars mendicant[150] continually present about the corpse, who sang masses and dirges for him without ceasing; about [...] were 24 great tapers, in goodly candlesticks of silver and over [...] the bed was an altar, whereupon from the break of day till 12 at noon, masses were continually sung; there was also a little chapel close by the room where the body lay, where in innumerable tapers and lights were burning. When the body was carried to be inhumed there went 24 friars with each a wax taper in his hand, that went encompassing the chariot and before it went 500 poor men by 2 and 2[151] in mourning apparel, every one of them bearing a torch lighted. Besides the court officers of the nobility and others of the French nobles, there were 11 cardinals who had numerous trains of attendants, and all in mourning. The funeral oration or sermon was pronounced by Peter Chastellan, who King Francis a little before his death had made Bishop of Macon. The Bishop among other things declared that the King was determined to found a college for 600 students wherein arts, sciences and languages should have been read and taught by Doctors and Masters in every faculty in places distinct and peculiar. For that purpose in the said college, and for the invitation and encouragement of the learned he had resolved to endow the same with an

---

[150] Original calls them 'begging friars'.

[151] 'By 2 and 2' does not appear in the original.

annual revenue of 50 thousand crowns for ever, firmly and legally assigned and established.

26.[152] Henry the 2 of that name King of France succeeded his father Francis the first and was crowned at Rheims, July 25th 1547 after this manner. The night before the day appointed for the solemnity, the King came to Rheims[153] and was received before the Cathedral Church by 3 cardinals, and so led to the High Altar, and after he had kissed there the relics of the saints enclosed in gold, and performed his private devotions in the Church he went to supper. And after supper he went again to the Church and said his prayers again and confessed himself to a priest. He returned back to his palace and went to bed. The next day he sent certain of the nobility to entreat the Abbot of St Remegius, that he would bring the vial of holy [...] which they say, came down from Heaven. Then resorted to the Church those that are called the 12 [...] of France [...] of Rheims [...] Novon and Chalon [...] of the Clergy, and [...] nobility, the King of Navarre, the Dukes of Vandosme, Guise, Nepers, Monpensier, and Albemarle. These last 6 rep[...] Dukes of Burgundy, Normandy Guinne, and the Earls of Flanders, Tholouse and Champagne. Of the Bishops, the Bishop of Langres and Beavois, and 2 Cardinals were chosen to go to fetch the King to the Cathedral. When they came into his chamber, they said certain prayers, the King yet in bed, and then as the ceremony is lift him up, and being apparelled led

---

[152] Sleidanus, p. 299.

[153] Rheims not mentioned in the original. This is an odd addition considering the faithful rendering of the rest of the passage.

him to Church accompanied with a multitude of priests, the constable carrying the sword drawn before him. The King coming thither was conducted to the altar, where having prayed before it, he was led by the Bishops to his seat, and in the mean time till the vial came, the Archbishop of the place (after he had finished the prayers contained in the Book of Ceremonies) sprinkled the King and all the rest with Holy Water; and when word was brought that the vial of oil was coming, which in the Abbot's absence at that time, the Prior of the monks brought, sitting upon a white ambling palfrey, accompanied with the monks of his order, and the noblemen the King had sent for it. Then the Archbishop went to the Church door, and there received the vial of the Prior delivering him a Gage to restore it to him again, and coming with it to the Altar, the King rising out of his seat doth him reverence. Then the Archbishop went into the vestry and there being solemnly arrayed in Pontificalibus,[154] he came to the King and took his oath and fidelity of him, by which after an ancient custom, Kings are bound to the Church. Then was the King led to the altar by two Bishops and their certain robes were put on him, then kneeling down, the Archbishop prepared him with a sword which he as they term it, had consecrated before with many prayers. After this the Archbishop prepared the oil in a readiness and while the priests sing their service, prayed softly with the King both lying grovelling on the ground. Then he anoints the King's head, breast, and both shoulders, and the elbows of either arms, saying the accustomed prayers. That done the King had new garments put on him

---

[154] That is, the robes or vestments of a Pope or Cardinal.

like a minister of the Church and then anointed on the palms of his hands; laying them on his breast, and then put on hallowed gloves. Then the Archbishop put a ring on his finger, and delivered him a sceptre in his right hand, and in the same moment the Chancellor called forth the 12 peers, and in their presence the Archbishop took from the altar the crown of Charles the great, and when the peers have touched it set it on the King's head, and then brought him to his Royal throne, which was erected in a higher place, the whole company of nobles following, and there having ended his prayers, kissed him. So do the peers and nobles and then a great shout and acclamation is made, crying aloud, God Save the King, and to rejoice men's hearts the trumpets blew, and gold and silver thrown among the people.[155] Then the Archbishop said Mass, and after the Gospel was read, the King went to the altar, and offered there certain pieces of gold, bread, and wine. And after the Mass was ended, received the Lord's Supper,[156] and then all went to dinner.

27.[157] Peter Aloise, the Bastard Son of Pope Paul III was a very lewd and wicked fellow, and several pamphlets were published in Italy of his insatiable[158] and detestable lusts, among the which is one that he forced and buggered Cosimo Cherie, Bishop of Essanen, by the aid of his servants, that held him, which filthy act so inwardly grieved the Bishop

---

[155] 'common people' in the original.

[156] 'after their manner' in the original

[157] Sleidanus, pp. 301-2.

[158] 'ungracious' in the original. The alteration makes Peter Aloise's reputation even worse.

that he died with sorrow and shame of the very thing. But some suppose that he was poisoned rather, that he should not discover that wretched act to the Emperor. The Pope[159] notwithstanding loved his son entirely, and applied himself to advance him to riches and honours[160] and as oft as he heard of his lewd pranks, he was not grieved there with at all, as was reported and would only say that he learned not these vices of him. The Pope then created his son Peter, Duke of Placentia and Parma, where he did many things contrary to the law and equity, and by his tyranny offended all sorts of men, among others he deprived Jerome Palavicine of all his lands and possessions who to eschew the danger threatened to his person, fled to Crema, a town belonging to the State of Venice, but his wife and children were cast into prison, and the proceeding against Palavicine by the Duke was like to stir up commotions against him, but the Cardinal of Trent thinking to prevent the worst, interposes in the business, and out of his love to the Pope and his family, writ to the Duke, but he had a froward answer. Octavius the Duke's son coming at the time to Trent, in his way homeward, to whom the Cardinal declares the whole matter concerning Palavicine, desiring him to be a petitioner to his father in his behalf. But Octavius either would not or could not do any thing though he had promised faithfully to the Cardinal that he would accomplish his desires, and when the Cardinal expected to hear of some real effects of Octavius his promise and being come with Palavicine to present him to the Duke, the Cardinal contrary

---

[159] 'Bishop' in the original, perhaps changed to clarify which 'bishop' was being discussed here.

[160] In the original only 'honour' is mentioned.

to what he expected, received a message in plain terms from the Duke that he cannot restore him, though the messengers sent by the Cardinal were both grave and understanding persons, and endeavoured to mitigate the Duke's fury. Wherefore the Cardinal seeing his endeavour come to nothing reconducted Palavicine safely to Crema, and so returned to Trent.

Before this tyrannical usage of Palavicine, certain of the discontented nobility and gentry subjects to the Duke who hated him also, considered his death, and having hired certain desperate murderers, waiting for a time only to execute their design, many times going abroad with these cut-throats attending them, each of them pretending to be in danger of private enemies; and in the mean time every of the malcontents sounded his hireling, whether they will faithfully take their part in revenging a wrong done unto them, as they said, by the Duke's steward who promise their service not only in this but also to kill the Duke himself. About the same time, the Pope his father, writes expressly to him, that he should look[161] to himself the 10th day of December for that the stars did prognosticate unto him, some great mischief that day. The Pope was much given not only to judicial astrology but to necromancy also, as many men affirmed, by which he foresaw the impending misfortune of his son.

When the Duke had received his father's letters, he was possessed with a fear and care of himself, and when that day was come he went out of the castle of Placentia,[162] in his

---

[161] 'take heed' in the original.

[162] 'of Placentia' added by commonplace author.

horse litter, with a great company attending him to view the new fortifications of the town he had begun. The Conspirators were there also, but when they could not then accomplish the thing desired they stay, and when he returned home, they waited on him, as it had been out of duty, go before him to the number of 36 and when he was come in his horse litter into the castle, some of the conspirators plucked up the drawbridge immediately, that no man should follow after, then with their swords drawn they approach to him, bitterly call him tyrant, and so with many wounds kill him in his litter, and at the same time murder his Chaplain, the Master of his Horse, and 5 Germans of his guard. After they run up and down the castle, and make spoil of all, finding much money and a great treasure, which he had amassed together for the fortification of the city, upon this there was a great concourse of people about the castle, inquiring what the matter was that they heard such a noise and crying within; answer was made from above, that they had killed the tyrant, and recovered the ancient liberty of the city but they within could hardly make the citizens believe the thing but when the citizens had warranted their lives, and they were assured of pardon, they hung out the dead body of the Duke by a chain on the wall, and after they had swung it to and fro a while, they let it fall into the ditch. Then the people ran to it, and stabbed it with their daggers, spurned it with their feet in despiteful manner, and left it mangled, torn and naked still in the ditch.

28.[163] Pope Paul the 3ᵈ who died anno 1549.aged 82 years and sat 15 years Pope[164] was very much afflicted for the death of his son Peter Aloise, murdered in the city of Placentia, of which place the Pope his father had put him in possession with the title of Duke. But because he conceived the Emperor had been some way privy to his son's death by reason that city was seized upon by Gonzaga for his use and would not restore it again to the Pope; he, if he had lived, would have taken the French King's part, as was thought purposely to be revenged, and nothing was more in his imagination than that. But before he left this life, then was published in Italian a virulent book against him, under the title of Barnadinus Ochinus, but compiled (as was thought) by others with a preface to Ascantus Colonna whom the Pope had banished. This book, among other things long and tedious to recite, as a learned author said, addresses his discourse to Paul himself, and first brands him with the title of Antichrist, and then proceeds to enumerate his horrible crimes in these downright terms.

You were, said Ochinus, in the time of Pope Innocent VIII committed to prison, a prelate most abominable for 2 detestable murders, and for paracide viz. for poisoning thy mother, and a nephew of thine, that the whole inheritance might descend unto you, and after being set at liberty you were so impudent as to sue for the red[165] hat thou being a man full of wickedness, but was thrice refused by the

---

[163] Sleidanus, p. 345.

[164] Contextual information added by commonplace author. Sleidanus's passage begins with his being upset at the death of Peter Aloise.

[165] Original 'purple'.

College of Cardinals, at last your sister[166] Julia Farnesta, a fine whore, obtained it for you for that she threatened the High Bishop, Pope Alexander VI that she would be no longer at his command, if thou was not made a Cardinal, so being afraid of her anger and displeasure, chose you into the fellowship of cardinals. After this you did also poison another sister that was more than half whorish, after the custom of thy family. When you were Nuncio[167] in the Province of Ancona, what time Julius 2 was Pope, full naughtily you did beguile a maid of the city, disguising yourself and making her believe that you were a Gentleman attending upon the Nuncio, and so deflowered her which shameful act the Maid's Uncle, the Cardinal of Ancona, charged you with boldly[168] before Pope Clement 7. Furthermore Nicholas Quercy took thee in wanton dalliance with his wife Laura Faresia, thy own niece, and gave you a gentle job[169] with his dagger, the scar whereof remains to this day. What should I speak of thy own daughter Constantia, with whom you have so often offended, and to the end that you might have her more freely at all times at thy pleasure, you didst poison her husband Boscus Sforza, but he escaped that villainy, yet perceiving thy great wickedness, and the mischief you didst prepare for him, he took such an inward thought, that he was never seen to be merry after. In filthy lusts, assuredly thou surpassed the

---

[166] Original 'your own natural sister'.

[167] Original 'ambassador'.

[168] Original 'earnestly'.

[169] i.e. jab. Appears as 'job' in both Sleidanus and commonplace book.

Emperor Commodus and Elagabulus[170] and that may be well proved by so many bastards as you have. Lot lay with his daughters ignorantly, and when he was made drunk, but thou o caitiff[171] meddled not only with thine own niece but also with thy own sister when you were sober.[172] Thou did cozen Pope Clement and made merchandise of the Church goods, when you were but cardinal, but since you were made Pope, living God, how filthily hast thou consumed the Church goods, in giving 40000 ducats yearly to Peter thy Bastard, and in maintaining the women of thy house, whores all, and in cheating all Christendom, under pretence of warfaring against the common enemy, and many such like pranks hast you played to all good men's grief, and shame to thy self.[173]
Is it not thou Pagan, a great misbelief in thee to depend upon astrology and necromancy, and to advance to riches and honours such as you can get that are skilful in these sciences, which thou, like an ungodly wretch as you are, well know to be taught never but in Belzebub's Academy, and is not this cause enough to depose thee and to sit thee beside the cushion and to heave thee out of the chair in which you sit to do the Devil's drudgery? Yes verily it is. There are many more such like things contained in the foresaid book, which was printed and published in the time even of Paul's Popeship, to which those that life may have recourse when they please.

---

[170] Second and third century Roman Emporers known for their immorality.

[171] 'O caitiffe' is inserted by commonplace author.

[172] Original says 'sister and daughter'.

[173] From here until the end of the paragraph does not appear in the original.

29.[174] In the Council of Trent November 25th 1551 the fathers being placed in their seats several decrees were recited among which was that touching penance, which runs thus: that penance is a sacrament instituted of Christ and necessary for such as after Baptism fall into sin again; that is also a several sacrament distinct from baptism, and as it were another table of salvation, after the shipwreck hath chanced. That the same words of Christ by which he gives to his Apostles the Holy Ghost ought to be understood of the power to forgive sins by the sacrament. That the sin should be forgiven, 3 things are required: contrition, confession and satisfaction and the contrition is a true and profitable sorrow which prepares a man unto grace. And confession or the manner secretly to recite the sins to the Priest, to be ordained by God's law and necessary to salvation. That all sins which come to remembrance and the circumstances of the same are to be rehearsed. That confession ought to be every year once at least and that chiefly in the time of Lent. That absolution is not a bare ministry, whereby the remission of sins is denounced but an act judicial. That priests only though they never be so sinful have authority to give absolution. Whereas bishops do reserve unto themselves certain cases and offences for the which other [...] can not afford to be well done. Although the crimes be remitted, yet is not the punishment thereby released. That satisfaction consists in work, and not in faith. That by such penance, as either God sendeth unto us, or the priest enjoys, or else of our own free will we choose unto ourselves, the sins are cleansed,

---

[174] Sleidanus, p. 340. This section is transcribed word for word.

concerning temporal punishment. That satisfactions whereby sins are redeemed, be God's service. That the Priest hath power to bind and loose. And therefore may enjoin penance to him that confesses his sins.

[175]The ceremonies of degrading a Priest, are then used in the Romish Church: [176] when a Priest is to suffer death, or utterly disabled from exercising the Priestly office and no other save Priests only, of all the rabble of religious persons in that hierarchy are degraded, which is done after this manner: when a priest is condemned of heresy by an ecclesiastical judge, he hath an alb and a vestment put upon him, and a chalice delivered into his hands, with wine and water also the gilt patten, with a single cake. And so kneeling upon his knees the Bishop's deputy takes from him some of the things before named, commanding him that he shall no more say mass for the quick and the dead. And with a piece of glass scrapes his fingers injoining him that he never here after hallow any thing; after he takes the rest of the things from him, with certain curses joined thereunto. When he is exempted thus out of the number of Priests, he is also put from the rest of the Orders, by the which he came unto Priesthood. Then he is stripped out of Priest's habit,[177] and attired again with a Lay-man's apparel, and so delivered to the Magistrate, who the Bishop's Chancellor entreats that he would determine no harm against his life nor body for they use this ceremony lest they being Holy Men, should seem to be the authors of death or bloodshed.

---

[175] Sleidanus, pp. 49-50.

[176] 'Romish church' does not appear in the original.

[177] 'torn naked' in the original.

30.[178] Maximilian, son to the Emperor Frederick III married Mary the inheritrix of Burgundy, by whom he had many rich countries, and brought him also a Son, called Philip; he married the Lady Jane, the daughter of Ferdinand King of Spain and had by her Charles and Ferdinand; when the Lady was first with child, she went into Flanders, and was brought a bed of Charles at Gaunt, Feb 24. 1500.[179] This Charles was chosen and declared King of the Romans after a stiff contest among the Electors, the Archbishop and Elector of Mentz, calling the nobility and common people into St Bartholomew's Church and in his sermon, declared Charles Archduke of Austria, and King of Spain to be King of the Romans instead of Maximilian deceased and exhorted them to give God thanks, and to show to him all fidelity and obeyance and speaking much in his praise, declared why the Electors chose him before all others and shortly after was elected Emperor in the same place according to the Canon Law of Pope Innocent III who lived about the year of our Lord 1200 which testifies, That [...] Princes Electors have free authority to create the Emperor. And that the Empire goeth not by Succession, but by Election.

[180]The Emperor elect, being come out of Spain into Flanders, and having set his affairs in order in the Low Countries, appointed the priests Electors to meet him at Acon October 6th to be inaugurated; but the Princes arriving

---

[178] First sentence here is contextual information added by commonplace author.

[179] Sleidanus, p. 20.

[180] Sleidanus, pp. 29-30.

in Colen 10 Miles from Acon, heard of a great Plague there whereupon they wrote to the Emperor being at Louvain, that he would choose some other place, but the Emperor sent the word that he could not so slightly break the law of Charles 4th which had so ordained it. Wherefore on the 21 of Oct: 1520 the 3 Ecclesiastical Electors came thither with the Duke of Saxonies and the Marquis of Brandenburg's Ambassadors. The next day they rode forth to meet the Emperor and lighting of their horses, received him very honourably by the mouth of my Lord of Mentz, which he answered gently by the Cardinal of Salzburg so joining together they marched towards the town. Before the gate the Pallgrave met him. The Electors had about 2500 Horse,[181] the Emperor 2000 all in gorgeous apparel; the Saxons and them of Cleve contested about precendency in so much that the Companies being great, it was night before they could enter into the town; on either side of the Emperor rode the 2 archbishops of Mentz and Collen; next after followed the King of Bohemia's Ambassador, 3 Cardinals and the Ambassadors of other Kings and Princes. The Pope's legate and the King of England's Ambassador were absent for some reasons about precedency. [182] The Emperor was brought in to our Lady's Church whereafter he had performed his orations he discoursed with the Elector apart and so went to his lodging. The next day, they met again at the church in the midst whereof hung a large crown, the floor underneath was covered with cloth of Arras; upon which the Emperor lay grovelling, whilst my Lord of Collen

---

[181] In the original 'some demilances and some archers'.

[182] Sleidanus explains that they were absent in case they had to appear in the procession after the Germans.

said certain prayers over him; which ended, the Archbishops of Mentz and Triers took him up and led him to our Lady's altar. Here he fell down again, and when he had prayed, he was led into his seat, which was richly gilt. Then the Archbishop of Collen began the Mass, and when he had proceeded a little, he demanded of him in Latin whether he will keep the Catholic faith, defend the Church, minister justice, restore the Empire, defend the Widowed, protect the fatherless, and relieve such as be in distress? Whether he will give due reverence to the Pope? After he hath assented, he was led to the Altar, and took his oath upon the same, and so returned to his seat again. After this the Archbishop of Collen asked the Princes whether they will give him their faith and allegiance? Which they promised, and certain prayers finished, he anoints the Emperor's breast, head and the boughs of his arms; this done the Archbishops of Ments and Triers led him to the vestry, and their being apparelled like a deacon, bring him again to his seat And after more prayers said, the Archbishop of Collen accompanied with the other two, delivered him a sword drawn, and commended the Common Wealth to him; and putting up the sword into the scabbard again, he put a ring upon his finger, and invested him with a robe royal. Then he put a sceptre in his hand, and an apple of gold representing the whole world; Then the 3 Archbishops together set the diadem upon his head, and so led him to the Altar, where he again did swear to do the duty of a good Prince. Afterwards they following him, conveyed him into an higher place, and set him in a seat of stone. There the Archbishop of Mentz speaking in the vulgar tongue wished him great prosperity commending unto him most diligently, himself and his peers, with all the states of the Empire. The like did the Prebends of the Church, the Emperor himself being by an old custom chosen a fellow of their College. When all is done, the trumpets blow a while;[183] when mass was done, the Emperor received the Lord's Supper, and dubbed as many knights as were willing. From the church they passed to the palace, most sumptuously hung and adorned, where the Emperor dined and the Electors also, every man at a table by himself. And the Archbishop of Triers was placed right over against the Emperor. According to the law of Charles 4th all the other tables were in the same hall on each side of the Emperor's table. That day, in an ancient custom, there was a whole ox roasted, with other beasts in his belly whole also:[184] a piece whereof was served up to the Emperor's table, all the rest was given to the common people: and all that day there ran 2 conduits with wine continually free for all men. After dinner the Emperor returned to his palace, where he delivered the seals of the empire to the Archbishop of Mentz. The next day he made a supper for the Priests Electors, and the day following the Emperor repaired again to Church: where he heard Mass and worshipped the relics of saints with great devotion,[185] among which was they said, a cloth that our Saviour was wrapped in, when he was in his swaddling clouts. After this the Archbishop of Mentz in the hearing of all the assembly, pronounced that the Pope approved this creation, and doth command him to use the name of Caesar.

---

[183] 'blow up mirth and melody' in the original. Other than this amendment, the original is copied exactly.

[184] 'farsed with other beasts' in the original.

[185] 'with great devotion' added by commonplace author.

31. Charles 5th (surnamed the Wise) King of France, gave the Dukedom of Burgundy (which fell unto him) to Philip his youngest Brother, with it the Lady Margaret the only daughter of Lewis Earl of Flanders. Which attribute of Wise Lewis then could never approve of in Charles, it being (as he said) very foolishly done to give away so rich a Dukedom as that of Burgundy to a younger brother, which donation was about the year 1470. This Philip had by his wife Margaret a son called John: and he had a son named Philip, who was father of Charles the Bold[186] who was slain before Nancy in a battle against the Swiss: leaving a daughter the inheritrix of many rich and large countries. She was married to Maximilian, son to the Emperor Frederick III and brought forth a son called Philip; He married the Lady Jane, the daughter of Ferdinand King of Spain and had by her Charles and Ferdinand: and when this Lady was great with her first child she went into Flanders, and was brought abed of Charles of Gaunt, Feb 24 1500.[187] The grandfather of this Charles by his mother's side was Ferdinand K. of Aragon and Sicily who had to wife Elizabeth, the daughter and heir of John II King of Spain and in time had also the Kingdom of Naples. He begat of her 5 children: John, Isabel, Jane, Mary and Katherin; John and Isabel having no issue of their bodies,[188] their inheritance by the laws of the realm came unto the next sister; By this means all that the Duke of

---

[186] 'Charles the stout warrior' in the original.

[187] Last three sentences are a copy of the section at the start of paragraph 30.

[188] 'dying without issue' in the original.

Burgundy had which was exceeding much and whatsoever Ferdinand King of Spain had, came wholly to Charles the son of the Lady Jane; For the lands of the House of Austria, in the division of the Inheritance, went to Ferdinand his brother. Wherefore a long time before his election, Germany had not an Emperor of greater power. His father died when he was but 6 years old, and his grandfather Ferdinand, when he was 16. at which time he went into Spain and there remained till he was elected Emperor, and went into Germany, which was in the year of our Lord 1520, he being just 20 years of age.

32.[189] At what time as the Pope Paul had prorogued the Council for Reformation anno 1538 to Vincentia in the state of Venice, he sent thither 3 Cardinals, Campeius, Simonet and Brundusium, which should both begin the Treaty and receive them that came. But the pope would have the matter of reformation kept close yet was the same not long hid, and when the book for reformation was brought from Rome, it was answered in the High Dutch tongue[190] by Luther, before which the Book of Luther's was set out a picture, which plainly emblematized[191] the argument for the Pope[192] was placed in a high seat, and certain cardinals standing about

---

[189] Sleidanus p. 164.

[190] 'Duche tongue' in original.

[191] 'declared' in the original.

[192] 'bishop' in the original.

him, who with fox tails tied to staves like besomes sweep all things topsy turvy,[193] upside down.

[194]And in the year 1545 Luther published another book in the vulgar tongue intituled 'Against the Bishop of Rome ordained by Satan' in the which book, he first answers the Pope's[195] letters wherein with vehement words he dissuaded the Emperor from the Reformation of religion. After, those places of scripture which the Pope doth write to establish his usurped supremacy, he confuted most amply, and applied them home to make against him; before this book he set a picture, which declared the whole sum of the argument: the Pope seated in a high chair with sundry shapes[196] some whereof were busy setting a triple crown upon head, with a goodly turd on the top of it, underneath the chair was hell, horrible to behold and others with cords letting him down thereunto, whilst some others brought wood and coals, and others as right gentle and serviceable devils stayed his feet, that he might descend rightly and softly.

[197]Soon after he set forth a picture only against the Pope a very fond one indeed it was (as they said)[198] but yet it was, as it were, a prophecy of some things to come and was this. The Pope in his prelates' apparel was set upon a great sow

---

[193] 'topsy turvy' has been inserted by the commonplace author.

[194] Sleidanus, p. 228

[195] 'Bishop's' in the original.

[196] 'devils of diverse shapes' in original. Omits comment in original that the Pope has 'ass's ears'.

[197] Sleidanus, p. 229.

[198] 'as they said' added by commonplace author. This is unusual as first person pronouns are usually purposely omitted by him.

with many dugs and with spurs on his heels [...] full sore on both sides therewith having the 2 fingers next the thumb of his right hand, stretched right up, as the manner is when he blesseth such as he chanceth to meet with. In his left hand he held a new smoking turd, at the smell whereof the sow lifts up her snout and with open mouth catcheth after her prey, but he in derision, blames her full bitterly saying, I will ride thee and spur thee too, whether thou wilt or no; thou hast troubled me long about a Council, that thee might raile on me at thy pleasure, and frankly accuse me: behold now, the same is that Council that the so greatly distrest. By this sow was signified Germany. These trifles of Luther's were scoffed at by divers[199] as unseemly from him, and not very modest; but he had his reasons why he did so, and was thought to have great foresight in things: for certainly there are divers and sundry things prophesied in his books whereof some proved true in the end, and the residue are as yet in the hands of God.

33.[200] The Bishop and Senate of Strasburg, an Imperial City, being at variance about Religion, the Bishop being a Papalian[201] and for that debarred the use of any of the Churches in the city which was wholly Lutheran. The Senate sent their Ambassador to the Emperor to abate the controversy, they had with their Bishop: wherefore by the Emperor's permission, there were certain arbitrators chosen

---

[199] 'many men taunted' in original.

[200] Sleidanus, p. 343. In this section the commonplace author does not substitute 'bishop' for 'Pope' as in previous sections.

[201] Word origin not found, meaning is 'Papist'.

for both parties, who being met in Oct: 1549 after long disputation, the Senate permitted 3 Churches for the Bishop to establish his Religion therein, and he to receive the clergy into his faithfulness and tuition and they to enjoy immunity and freedom, paying the Senate a yearly tribute, and the Bishop again covenanted and granted to the Senate the College of St. Thomas: for [....] school and the rest of the Churches. The matter being thus taken[202] Cardinal Pool being sent for into England by King Phillip and Queen Mary, came accordingly and had come sooner but that the Emperor Charles 5th fearing he might prove a corrival[203] with his son Philip, had used means to stop his passage, but his son's marriage being past, he was content to let him pass; who thought he came from Rome, with a great authority of a Legate and Latere, yet he would not but come privately into London, because his Attainder was yet upon record. An Act therefore was presently passed to take it off, and to restore him in blood; for passing of which act, the King and Queen came in person to the Parliament house, whither a few days after: the Cardinal came himself, which was then kept in the great Chamber of Whitehall, because the Queen by reason of sickness was not well able to go abroad, and here the King and Queen sitting under the cloth of estate, and the card: on their right hand, all the Lords, Knights, and Burgesses being present, the Bishop of

---

[202] Sleidanus, pp. 445-446. Omits detail about Pole coming from Brabant, and his disagreement with Charles the Holy Roman Emperor. This is unusual as text suddenly changes topic from Strasburg to Queen Mary.

[203] That is, rival.

Winton,[204] Lord Chancellor made a short speech unto them all, signifying this presence of the Lord Cardinal and that he was sent from the Pope as his Legate and Latere, to do a work tending to the glory of God, and the benefit of them all, which (said he) you may better understand from his own mouth; Then the Cardinal rose up and made a long solemn oration, where he first thanked them for his restoring, by which he was enabled to be a member of their society; then exhorting them to return into the bosom of the Church for which end he was come; not to condemn, but to reconcile; not to compel but to require: and for their first work of reconciliation requiring them to repeal and abrogate all such laws as had formerly been made in derogation of the Catholic religion after which speech, the Parliament[205] going together, drew up a supplication, which within 2 days after they presented to the King and Queen wherein they showed themselves to be very penitent for their former errors and humbly desired their Majesties to intercede for them to the Lord Cardinal and the See Apostolic, that they might be pardoned of all they had done amiss, and be received into the bosom of the Church being themselves most ready to repeal all Laws unjudicial to the See of Rome. This supplication being delivered to the Cardinal he then gave them absolution in these words, We by the Apostolic Authority given to us by the most Holy Lord Pope Julius III (Christ's vicegerent on earth) do absolve and deliver you and every of you, and the whole realm and dominions thereof from all heresy and schism, and from all judgements,

---

[204] i.e. the Bishop of Winchester.

[205] In the original 'the nobility and commons'. This change shows the post-civil war view of the commonplace author.

censures, and pains for that cause incurred, and also we do restore you again, to the unity of our mother the holy Church. The report hereof coming to Rome, was cause that a solemn procession was made, for joy of the conversion of England to the Church of Rome.[206]

[207]Taken up by the arbitrament,[208] the Bishop intended to introduce the Mass in his Churches, at Christmas, and had prescribed the clergy an order which they were to follow; but for that they were not fully furnished he deferred it to the 1 of January 1550. Then, in those temples, the Priests began, first to sing their evensong, and the next day Mass, which for the space of 21 years had been prohibited,[209] at which there was a great concourse of people, especially the younger sort, for it was a strange site unto them, and never heard of before to see so many shaven crowns, and in a strange kind of apparel; who said[210] that which none of them understood; tapers and lamps burning at noon days; smoking and fuming with censors; then to see the Priest and his assistants standing at the altar pronouncing all things in a strange language; using many duckings[211] and sundry other gestures; bowing down with his hands fast closed; one while casting his arms abroad, another while bringing in the same;

---

[206] Sleidanus, pp. 317-318. This section is not copied out word for word, but follows the same basic pattern: a discussion of Pole's exhortation, Parliament's response and Pole's enunciation of the Papal Bull.

[207] Text suddenly reverts to Strasburg narrative. Sleidanus pp. 348-349.

[208] i.e. 'the decision'.

[209] 'omitted' in the original.

[210] 'sang' in the original.

[211] 'curtsies' in the original.

sometimes turning himself about, now crying aloud and now again muttering something in great secrecy, sometimes looking up aloft, sometime down to the ground; not standing still in a place but removing now to the right hand, and then again to the left hand of the altar, to cross and bless with his fingers, to breath in the chalice; to knock on his breast with his fist; to sigh; to wink as though he were asleep and then again to stare with them; to eat one part of the Bread; and sup of the rest of the wine, least one crumb or any one drop should remain; to wash his hands; to cross and bless with a gilt patten and to put the same to his forehead; to kiss one while at the altar, another while an image standing thereon, enclosed in timber or metal, in certain places to name one while the living, another while the dead; these things and such like the young people beheld not without great marvel and wonder, and certainly not without some laughter and so could hardly be restrained[212] by some graver persons among them from putting some affronts upon the Priests or in a jeering manner to taunt at their mimical gestures.

34.[213] The fathers in the Council of Trent were not unanimous and drew not all by one Cord; the Spanish Bishops indeed of all the others deemed most diligent: divers also of the German Bishops pretended as though the abuses and errors crept into the Church both in discipline and doctrine required much Reformation but the Italian Bishops being the Pope's creatures said and did nothing but

---

[212] Rest of this section added by commonplace author to further illustrate common people's humour at Catholic ritual.

[213] Sleidanus, p. 396.

as they were influenced by his Legates, who prescribed therein. But the minds of them that thought best of all others was this: that the school of correction and manners of the Church should be reformed, that all superfluous excess, ambition and dishonest examples of living should be taken away, that every man be resident in his own Church and that each man should have one Benefice, and no man to be permitted to have more. Furthermore the same well minded persons purposed also to restrain and limit within certain boundaries the power of the Pope, and not to attribute to his court at Rome so great authority over all kingdoms. These and other such like things they comprised by this word 'reformation' and these things all the fathers did claim and acknowledge to belong properly to them. But as touching matters of religion and doctrine, they would acknowledge no error yea and that Councils could not err; and verily thought that their adversaries would in time recant, and submit to the decrees of the Council, which opinion and hope was increased for that they judged there were but few Professors of that doctrine left which impugned theirs, many of them being dead or banished. This was also common among them that whatsoever concerned Religion should easily and speedily be determined. The fathers in a late Council held at Basil in Switzerland submitted their judgement to Holy Scripture and to other writings agreeable to the same. But these men would be judges themselves in expounding the Scripture and follow the traditions of the Apostles in every doubtful matter, and whensoever they were destitute of scriptures to prove the truth of their doctrine, they boasted that it was so left by the Apostles and delivered unto them from hand to hand, which traditions of the Apostles the

Protestants say, are to be understood to be only those writings which were annexed to the New Testament or the sacred story of the 4 Evangelists.

[214]35. In the first year of the reign of Queen Mary anno 1554 Cardinal Pool was sent into England by Pope Julius III with authority as Legate to absolve the Kingdom, and a Parliament being begun the 12 of November in the same year, and the Cardinal come into Brabant, certain persons were sent to conduct him, and amongst them the Lord Paget. The 24th of November he came to London being right honourably received in all places wheresoever he came, and was immediately restored to his blood and inheritance,[215] with common assent and consent, from that which King Henry VIII displaced him. The 5th day after he came into the Parliament house and in the presence of King Philip and Queen Mary, who had intermarried before July 19[216] when he had showed the Parliament cause of his Legation, he exhorted them to return to the communion of the Church and to restore to the most holy father the Pope, his due authority, who will grant unto them all clemency and favour,[217] he admonished them also to give God thanks; who had given them such a King and Queen where as they have restored him to his house and inheritance, he taketh it for a very great benefit, and sayeth he is so much the more bounden, to

---

[214] Sleidanus, p. 445. Similar to middle section of paragraph 33, but much closer to original.

[215] 'house of inheritance' in the original.

[216] Section on their marriage date not included in original.

[217] 'gentleness' in original.

restore them again to the heavenly court and possession, which he unfainedly wished them above all other things and when he had thus, he retired out of the Parliament house.

Then the Bishop of Winchester being Chancellor repeated the Cardinal's speech, and with many words exhorted the Parliament to unity and concord and telling them that they are bound to give God thanks, who of his unspeakable mercy hath raised them up a prophet of their own seed which is that most illustrious[218] Cardinal, which is wholly inclined to their salvation.

The next day, when the nobility and Commons of both Houses had approved of the speech and requests of Cardinal Poole they drew up a petition and presented the same by their respective members to the King and Queen wherein they humbly beseeched their Majesties that they would intercede for them to him. The sum of which supplication was that it repenteth them much, for their late schism for that they have deemed obedience to the Apostolical Seat and that they have consented to such Acts and Decrees made against the same; but from henceforth they will be at the commandment of him and the Queen and will do all that ever they can that all such Laws and Statutes may be abrogated this same Parliament; wherefore they most humbly beseech their Highnesses that they would be a means and bring to pass, that being absolved from their sins, which they have committed against the Laws of the Church, and of the censures they have incurred for the same, they may be received again as penitent children in the body[219] of

---

[218] 'honourable' in original.

[219] 'bosom' in the original.

Christ's Church that from henceforth they may serve God in the obedience of the See and Bishops of Rome, to the glory of his holy name, and increase of their own salvation. Another day when the King and Queen and the Lord Cardinal Pool were present. The Chancellor stood up and openly pronounced what the States had determined concerning the request of his Holiness's Legate;[220] afterward he exhibited the supplication and petition aforesaid, written and subscribed to the King and Queen beseeching them to receive it which they did and when they had opened it, delivered it again to the Chancellor to read; then having read it he demanded of all the members if they be content there with which when they had affirmed the King and Queen arose and delivered it to the Cardinal. Then was the same read again that all men might perceive that he had authority[221] given him by the Pope to absolve them. After he had made another speech declaring how acceptable a thing repentance is to God and how much the angels in heaven rejoice for a penitent sinner, alleging for that purpose many examples giving God thanks who had put in them hearts desirous of amendment. This done, the Cardinal stood up, so did the King and Queen and kneeling all 3 on their knees the Cardinal calling upon the high power and mercy of God besought him to look mercifully upon this people, and to pardon their offences; and affirming himself to be sent for that purpose from the High Bishop to the multitude and atoned them. After this they went to the Chapel where thanks was given to God, then did the organs play, the

---

[220] Original 'the Bishop of Rome's'.

[221] Original 'letters of commission'.

trumpets sound and all tokens else of mirth and gladness were showed, as at such times is accustomed. They that knew Cardinal Pool before marvelled much at these his doings for by his talk and manner of living other manner of stuff was looked for at his hands by them.

[222] About the middle of January 1555 the Parliament broke up and among other acts, an Act passed for the restoring of Cardinal Pool and the Acts of former Kings concerning the punishing of Heretics and authority of Bishops were renounced but chiefly the Pope's supremacy was entirely restored and all the Laws and Statutes that had been made against the See of Rome, by the space of 20 years were utterly abolished and made void,[223] and it was also determined that extraordinary ambassadors should be sent to Rome in the name of the whole realm, to give his Holiness[224] thanks for his great clemency which he had showed towards them, and to promise him from henceforth all duty,[225] obedience and fidelity.

---

[222] Sleidanus, p. 446 (later after a break). Section omitted by commonplace author concerns the orders from the Emperor in the same year.

[223] Original 'condemned and abolished'. A section in the original is here omitted about the hopes that Philip would be crowned and on the conviction of heretics.

[224] Original 'the bishop'.

[225] 'duty' does not appear in the original.

36.[226] There are 2 actions[227] related of King Edward the Confessor the 14th monarch of the Saxons, who began his reign anno 1045 and reigned 24 years[228] that seem nothing correspondent to the general opinion had of his virtue, the one concerning his mother, the other touching his wife. That concerning his mother Emma was this. That because after King Ethelred's death she married the Danish King Canutus and seemed to favour her issue by him, more than her issue by King Ethelred, therefore he dispossessed her of all her goods and committed her to custody in the Abbey of Worwell and more than this so far hearkened to an aspersion cast upon her, of unchaste familiarity with Alwin, Bishop of Winton, that for her purgation she was fain to pass the Trial of Fire ordeal, which was in this manner: 9 Plough Shares red hot were laid in unequal distance, which she must pass over barefoot and blindfold and if she pass them unhurt then was she adjudged innocent, if otherwise, guilty. And this trial she passed and came fairly off to the great astonishment of all beholders.

The other touching his Wife was this. He had married Editha the beautiful and indeed virtuous daughter of the Earl Goodwyn, and because he had taken displeasure against the father he would show no kindness to the daughter, he had made her his wife but conversed not with her as his wife,

---

[226] A new book is used for the first time since paragraph 15: Richard Baker, *A Chronicle of the Kings of England* (London, 1643) p. 19.

[227] 'acts' in the original.

[228] This section of contextual information about Edward the Confessor is added by the commonplace author. Otherwise this paragraph is a word for word copy.

only at board he did, but not in bed; or if in bed it was no otherwise, then David with Abishag[229] and yet was content to hear her accused of incontinency whereof if she were guilty he could not be innocent. So, with that, for which after his death he should be reputed a saint, does not easily appear. It seems he was pious but not without ungratefulness to his mother, chaste but not without injury to his wife, his mother.[230] Queen Emma in memory of the 9 plough shares she had passed in her trial, gave 9 manors to the Minister of Winchester, and himself remembering the wrong he had done her bestowed on the same place the island of Portland in Dorsetshire, being about 7 miles in compass. Just in his present Government but not without neglect of posterity for through his want of guidance in that point, he left the crown to so doubtful succession that soon after his death it was translated out of English into French, and the kingdom made servile to a 4th foreign nation.

37.[231] King Richard I of that name after the funeral of Henry II his father who died in Normandy anno 1189[232] and was buried at Fonteverard in France: went to Roan, where he settled the state of that province and from thence came into

---

[229] Abishag was a beautiful young woman who was servant to the elderly KingDavid. Although she shared a bed with the King, they did not consummate the relationship. (see I Kings 1:4).

[230] The next sentence is not present in the original. The theme of nine manors to commemorate her sins comes from somewhere else, a manuscript source perhaps.

[231] Baker, p. 48. This section is almost a direct copy.

[232] Original says only 'after his Fathers funeral'. Contextual information added by commonplace author.

England and was crowned at Westminster by the hands of Baldwin Archbishop of Canterbury September 3 in the same year and herein the prince is more beholding to writers then any of his predecessors; for in speaking of their crowning they content themselves with telling where on and by whom they were crowned; But of this Prince they declare the manner of his Coronation in the full amplitude of all circumstances, which perhaps is not unfit to do, for satisfaction of such as are never like to see a Coronation and it was in this manner.

First the Archbishops of Canterbury, Roan, Trier, and Dublin with all the other bishops, Abbots and clergy apparelled in rich copes and having the cross, holy water and censors carried before them come to fetch him at the door of his privy chamber and receiving him, they led him to the Church of Westminster, with a solemn procession till they came before the high altar. In the middle of the bishops and clergy went 4 Barons bearing candlesticks with tapers; after which came Geoffrey de Lucy bearing the Cap of Maintenance and John Marshall next to him bearing a large pair of spurs of massive gold. Then followed William Marshal, Earl of Strigule, alias Pembroke, who bare the Royal Sceptre, on the top whereof was set a cross of gold and William de Patrick, Earl of Salisbury going next him, bear the Warder or Rod having on the top thereof a dove. Then came 3 other Earls, David Earl of Huntingdon, Brother to the King of Scots; John Earl of Mortaine, the King's Brother and Robert Earl of Leicester each of them bearing a sword upright in his hand, with the scabbards richly adorned with gold the Earl of Mortaigne went in the midst between the others, after them followed 6 Earls and Barons bearing a checker [...] upon the which were set the King's Escutcheons of Arms; then follows William Mandevile, Earl of Albemarle bearing a crown of gold a great height next before the King who followed having the Bishop of Durham on the right hand, Reynold, Bishop of Bath on the left: over which a canopy was borne, and in this order they came into the Church at Westminster where before the high altar in the presence of the clergy and the people laying his hand upon the Holy Evangelists and the relics of certain saints he took a solemn oath. That he should observe peace, honour and reverence to almighty God, to his Church and to his Ministers, all the days of his life. Also that he should exercise upright justice to the people committed to his charge; and that he should abrogate and disannul all evil laws and wrongful customs, if any were to be found in the precinct of his realm and maintain those that were good and laudable. This done he put off all his garments from his middle upwards, but only his shirt which was open on the shoulders, that he might be anointed; then the Archbishop of Canterbury anointed him in 3 places on the head on the shoulders and on the right arm, with prayers in such case accustomed. After this he covered his head with a linen cloth hallowed and set his cap thereon, and then after he had put on his Royal garments and his uppermost robe, the Archbishop delivered him the sword with which he should beat down the enemies of the Church which done 2 Earls put his shoes upon his feet, and having his mantle put on him, the Archbishop forbad him on behalf of Almighty God, not to presume to take upon him the dignity, except he faithfully meant to perform those things which he had there sworn to perform: whereunto the King made answer, that by God's grace he would perform them. Then the King took the crown beside the altar and delivered it to the Archbishop which he set upon the King's head, delivering to him the sceptre to hold in his right hand and the Rod Royal to hold in his left hand, and thus being crowned, he was brought back by the bishops and Barons, with the cross and candlesticks, and 3 swords passing forth before him unto his seat. When the Bishop that sung the Mass came to the Offertory, the 2 bishops that brought him to the Church led him to the altar and brought him back again; the Mass ended, he was brought with solemn procession back into his chamber and this was the manner of this King's Coronation.

[233]In the 22th year of the reign of King Henry VII[234] he began to be troubled with the gout, but a defluxion also falling[235] into his breast, wasted his lungs, so that thrice in a year and especially in the Spring he had great labouring in fits of Physic,[236] which brought him to his end, at his Palace at Richmond April 22th 1508, when he had lived 52 years, and reigned 23 and 8 months. Being dead, and all things necessary for his funeral pomp prepared, his corpse was brought out of the privy chamber into the great chamber where it rested 3 days; and every day, had there a Mass and a Dirge said by a prelate, mitred; and from thence it was conveyed into the hall: where it remained also 3 days, and had a like daily service there of Masses and Dirges, and likewise the same in the chapel, for other 3 days. Then upon

---

[233] Baker, p. 179.

[234] Name of king inserted by commonplace author for clarity.

[235] 'taking' in the original.

[236] 'Tissick' in the original. 'Fissick' in the commonplace manuscript.

Wednesday May 9th the corpse was put into a chariot, and over the corpse, was an effigy[237] of the deceased King, laid upon cushions of Cloth of Gold; and the effigies was arrayed in the King's richest robes, with a crown on his head, and a ball, and sceptre in his hands. When the chariot was thus ordered, the gentlemen of the King's Chapel, and a great number of prelates set forward, praying: then followed all the King's servants in black. After them followed the chariot 9 mourners, and on every side were carried torches by persons clad in black, to the number of 600 and in this order they came from Richmond to St. George's Fields in Southwark, where there with all the priests and religious men within the City of London and without: the Mayor and Aldermen, with many Commoners of the best rank, all clothed in black, met the corpse at London Bridge; and so the chariot was brought through the city to the Cathedral Church of St Paul, where the body was taken out, and carried into the Quire, and set under a stately hearse[238], where after solemn Mass was sung,[239] a sermon was preached[240] by the Bishop of Rochester. The next day, the corpse in a like processional manner was conveyed to Westminster, Sir Edward Howard bearing the King's Banner. In the Church was a curious hearse full of lights, which were all lighted at the coming of the corpse. Then was the corpse taken out of the chariot at the Church door[241] by 6

---

[237] 'picture' in the original.

[238] 'goodly hearse of wax' in the original.

[239] 'was sung' inserted here.

[240] 'made' in the original.

[241] 'at the church door' added by commonplace author.

Lords, and set under the hearse, which was double railed; when the mourners were all set, Garter Knights at Arms cried aloud 'For the Soul of the Noble Prince King Henry VII late King of this Realm'. The next day 3 masses were solemnly sung by Bishops and after they were ended, the King's Banner,[242] his Coat of Arms, Sword, target and Helmet were offered and at the end of another Mass, the mourners offered up rich palls of Cloth of Gold and bodkin; and when the choir sang 'Libera Me', the body was put into the earth; then the Lord Treasurer, Lord Steward, Lord Chamberlain, the Treasurer, and Comptroller brake their staves and cast them into the grave. Then Garter cried with a loud voice, 'Vive Le Roy, Henry le huitissime; Roy d'Angleterre et de France, Syre d'Irlande'. And thus ended the funeral.

39.[243] William the Conqueror, who though he were a conqueror of men, was yet conquered himself by death, on the 9th of September in the 64th year[244] of his age, when he had reigned near 21 years, and well may it be said[245] he was conquered by death seeing death used him more despitefully, than ever he living used any which he conquered; for no sooner was the breath out of his body, but his attending servants purloining what they could lay hands on, forsook him and fled, leaving his body almost naked

---

[242] 'Banner and Courser' in the original.

[243] Baker, p. 27.

[244] 'three score and fourth year' in the original.

[245] 'I may well say' in the original.

upon the ground; afterwards William Archbishop of Roan, commanded his body should be conveyed to Caen. But in this his command was little regarded, till at last one Herlewyne a Country Knight, at his own charges caused his body to be embalmed and conveyed thither: where the Abbot and Monks meeting the corpse, suddenly in the midst of their solemnities a violent fire brake out in the town, with the fright whereof every man left the place, thus was his body left a second time forlorn. In the end a few monks returned, and accompanied the hearse to the Abbey Church but when the Divine office was ended, and the body ready to be laid in the grave, one Anselme Fitz Arthur stood up and claimed that ground to have been[246] the floor of his father's house, which King William had violently wrested from him and thereupon charged that as they would answer it before the dreadful face of God, not to cover his body with the earth of his inheritance, whereupon after some pause, agreement was made with him and three pounds was paid in hand for the ground broken up and one hundred pounds more afterward for the ground itself paid him by Henry the King's youngest son, who only of all his sons was present at the funeral. And yet this was not all, for when the body was to be put into the earth, it happened that the sepulchre of stone which stood within the grave, was hewn somewhat too straight for his fat belly, so that they were fain to press it down into it with some violence, with which his bowels burst, or whether some excremental matter[247] were forced out of its natural passage, such an intolerable stink

---

[246] 'beene' in original; 'bin' in manuscript.

[247] 'excrements' in the original.

proceeded from him, that none there were able to endure it but made all the haste they could to be gone. And yet neither was this the last of his miseries, for in the year 1562 when Chastilion took the City of Caen, certain dissolute soldiers opened his tomb and not finding any treasure there they expected, they threw forth his bones in great derision. Some whereof were afterward bought into England; so that if the many troubles in his life, and even after his death be considered[248] this deduction may be drawn. That not withstanding all his grandeur,[249] a very mean man would hardly be persuaded to change fortune with him.

40.[250] The Bishop of Ross being Ambassador in England from Mary Queen of Scots, and after her expulsion out of Scotland and coming into England, he as the Scottish Queen's Delegate was discovered to be guilty of several sinister practices, and the whole contriver of some dangerous intended disturbances against the person of Queen and State of England.[251] Wherefore Queen Elizabeth caused her council to convene, who being made acquainted with Ross his actions, it was deliberated among them what to do with him, because he was an Ambassador. Hereupon, diverse learned[252] civilians were called, as Dr David Lewis, Dr

---

[248] 'if we consider' in the original.

[249] 'greatness' in the original.

[250] Baker, p. 249.

[251] This sentence added as contextual information by the commonplace author.

[252] 'learned' added by commonplace author.

Valentine Dale, and William Drury, William Aubny, and Henry Jones, bachelors, of whom these Questions were asked.[253] First, whether an Ambassador who raiseth rebellion against that Prince to whom he is an Ambassador may enjoy the privileges of an Ambassador, and is not liable to punishment? They answer'd that such an Ambassador hath forfeited the privileges of an Ambassador, and is liable to punishment. Secondly, whether the Minister or Proctor of a Prince, who is deposed by public authority and in whose room another is inaugurated may enjoy the privileges of an Ambassador? They answered that if such Prince be lawfully deposed his Proctor cannot challenge the privileges of an Ambassador, forasmuch as none but absolute Princes, and such as have right of Majesty can appoint Ambassadors. Thirdly, whether a Prince who is come into another Prince's country, and held in custody may have his Proctor, and if he shall be held an Ambassador? They answered if such a Prince have not lost his sovereignty, he may have his Proctor; but whether that Proctor shall be reputed an Ambassador or no, this depends[254] upon the authority of his delegation. Fourthly, whether if a Prince give warning to such a Proctor, and to his Prince, who is under custody, that his Proctor shall not from henceforth be accounted for an Ambassador, whether that Proctor may by law challenge the privilege of an Ambassador? They answered a Prince may forbid an Ambassador to enter into his Kingdom, and may command him to depart the Kingdom, if he contain not

---

[253] These questions copied out word for word.

[254] 'dependeth' in the original, 'depends' in the commonplace book. This shows an inconsistency, the author sometimes modernising language and sometimes copying word for word.

himself within his due limits; yet in the mean while he is to enjoy the privileges of an Ambassador?

Upon these answers, the Bishop of Ross was[255] warned by the Lords of the Council that he should no longer be esteemed an ambassador, but be punished as his fault did deserve. The Bishop alleged for himself that he had not violated the right of an Ambassador, Via Juris but Via Facti (which were his own words) and therefore advised them not to use harder measure to him than was used to the English Ambassadors, Throgmorton[256] in France and Randall and Tamworth in Scotland, who had raised rebellions and were open abettors of the same[257]; and tried against him; he lovingly requested them to give no credit to it; for as much as by a received custom, which hath the force of a law, the testimony of an Englishman against a Scot, or of a Scot against an Englishman is not to be admitted, but after some other altercations, the Bishop was[258] sent away to the Tower and kept close prisoner.

41.[259] The Lords of the Privy Council to Queen Elizabeth[260] being at difference amongst themselves by what Law to

---

[255] 'is' in the original.

[256] The name Throgmorton does not appear in the original.

[257] Original mentions that their punishment was banishment but nothing further.

[258] Again, original uses the historical present tense here.

[259] Baker, p. 269.

[260] 'them' in the original. Commonplace author adds contextual information again.

proceed against the Queen of Scots[261] whether by the law of 25th of Edward III in which they are pronounced guilty of Treason, who plot the destruction of the King or Queen raise war in his Dominions, or adhere to his Adversaries, or else by the 27 of the Queen, enacted a year before: their opinion at last prevailed who thought best to proceed against her by the latter law, as being indeed in the case provided whereupon divers of the Lords of the Privy Council and others of the Nobility, are authorised by the Queen's letters to enquire by virtue of that law and to pass sentence against all such as raised rebellion, invaded the Kingdom, or attempted any violence against the Queen. These Commissioners therefore Oct 11th repaired to Fotheringay Castle in Northamptonshire, where the Queen of Scots was then a prisoner, and the next day, sent Sir Walter Mildmay, Sir Amias Pawlet and Edward Barker a public notary who delivered her the Queen's letters, which having with a settled countenance read, she said, it seems strange to me that the Queen should lay her command upon me, to hold my hand at the Bar as though I were a subject since I am an absolute Queen, no less than her self; but howsoever I will not do any thing prejudicial to Princes of my degree, nor to my son the King of Scotland.

After many meetings, she insisting[262] still upon her innocence, and upon her exemption from answering as being an absolute Prince and specially for yielding to be tried by the English Laws; of which one (she said) had lately been[263]

---

[261] 'her' in the original.

[262] 'standing' in the original.

[263] 'bin' in commonplace book.

made of purpose for her destruction. At last she was told her plainly, by the Lord Chancellor Bromeley[264] and by the Lord Treasurer that if she refused to answer to such crimes as should be objected, they would then proceed against her though she were absent; being brought at last with much ado to consent the Commissioners came together in the Presence Chamber, a chair of state[265] was set forth for the Queen of England in the upper end of the Chamber, under a canopy, and beneath over against it, was placed a chair for the Queen of Scots; on both sides of the cloth of estate, stools were set upon which on the one side sat the Lord Chancellor, [266]the Earls of Oxford, Kent, Darby, Worcester, Rutland, Cumberland, Warwick, Pembroke, Lincoln, and Viscount Mountacute; on the other side the Lords Aburgaveny, Zouch, Morly, St. John of Bletso, Compton, and Cheney; next to these sat the Knights that were Privy Counsellors, Sir James Crofts, Sir Christopher Hatton, Sir Francis Walsingham, Sir Ralph Sadler, Sir Walter Mildmay, and Sir Amias Pawlet forward before the Earls sat the 2 Chief Justices and the Lord Chief Baron; on the other side, the other Justices and the other Barons; in the midst at a table sat Dr Dale and Dr Ford, Drs of the Civil Law, and Popham, the Lord Attorney General Egerton, her solicitor Gawdy, her sergeant at Law, the Clerk of the Crown, and 2 Notaries.

When the Queen of Scots was come, and had placed her self, silence being made, the Lord Chancellor turning towards her

---

[264] Name not in original.

[265] 'estate' in the original.

[266] This list copied exactly apart from the omission here of the Lord Treasurer.

said that the Queen had appointed these Commissioners to hear what she could answer to crimes laid to her charge, assuring her that nothing would be cause of more joy to the Queen than to hear that she had proved herself innocent. Upon this she rising up protested her innocence, she was now content to appear;[267] then Sergeant Gawdy opened every specialty of the law late made (against which she had taken exception) showing, by Babington's confessions, by letters passed between them, by the confessions of Bullard, and Savage and also by the confessions of her secretaries, Nurse and Curle, that she was privy to the treasons and consented to the invasion of England and destruction of the Queen to which she answered, that letters might be counterfeited, her secretaries might be corrupted, the rest in hope of life, might be drawn to confess that which was not true but in this she stood peremptorily, that she never consented to any attempt against the Queen's person; though for her own delivery she confessed she did; after many other charges urged by the Commissioners against her and her replies, at last she requested that she might be heard in a full Parliament or before the Queen herself and her Council. But this request prevailed not. For on the 25th October following, at the Star chamber[268] the Commissioners met again, and there pronounced sentence against her, ratifying by their seals and subscriptions, that after the 2 day of June, in the 27th year of our Sovereign Lady Queen Elizabeth divers

---

[267] The original transcribes a sentence or two of Mary, Queen of Scots' words but omitted by commonplace author. Perhaps this is because he is keen to read on quickly to the dramatic section discussing her conviction and execution.

[268] Original adds 'at Westminster'.

matters were imagined in this Kingdom, by Anthony Babington, and others with the privity of Mary Queen of Scots, pretending title to the crown of England tending to the hurt, death and destruction, of the Royal Person of our said Sovereign Lady the Queen. Soon after the sentence passed upon the Queen of Scots was confirmed by Parliament [crossed out material][269] which being prorogued, the Lord Buckham, and Mr Beale Clerk of the Council were sent to the Queen of Scots to let her understand that sentence was pronounced against her, and confirmed by Parliament and that the execution of it was earnestly desired by the Nobility and Commons, and therefore persuaded her, that before her death she would acknowledge her offences against God, and the Queen intimating that if she had lived, the religion received in England could not subsist.

The Queen of Scots was hereupon taken with an unwonted alacrity, and seemed to triumph for joy, giving God thanks and congratulating for her own felicity. That she should be accounted an instrument for the establishing religion in England[270] and there with requested, she might have some

---

[269] Large section from the original omitted here regarding Parliament's censure of the accomplices and seizure of their property. Parliament tried to persuade Elizabeth of the dangerous Biblical precedents of failing to execute one's enemies. Elizabeth responded that she was not happy about the law being used for the death of another queen and she asked for time to think. 12 days later she asked for some consideration of some way in which Mary might be spared. But she was told that her life would not be safe until Mary was dead or unless she acknowledged her crimes and was kept in permanent custody. Reluctantly Elizabeth told Parliament that she knew she had to be cruel in this case and do what they wanted. The commonplace author then starts to take notes again. The crossed out section of two and a half lines indicates that he had begun to take notes from this missing section and then changed his mind.

[270] 'in this island' in the original.

catholic priest to administer the sacrament to her, but was denied which to her[271] she utterly rejected them and jeered at the English nation, saying the English were ever and anon wont to murder their own Kings and therefore, no marvel they should now thirst after her destruction. In December following the sentence against her was proclaimed in London first after over all the Kingdom, wherein Queen Elizabeth seriously protested that the promulgation of the sentence was extorted from her, to her great grief, by the importunity of the whole body of the Kingdom. The Queen of Scots being told hereof, seemed not a whit dejected with it; but writing to the Queen never made intercession for herself, nor expostulated her death, but only made 3 final[272] requests; one that she might be buried in France by her mother; another, that she might not be put to death, privately, but her servants to be present; the third that her servants might freely depart, and enjoy such legacies as she had given them. Of which requests, she desired the Queen to vouchsafe her an answer, but whether this letter ever came to her[273] hands is uncertain.

[274]Queen Elizabeth deeply weighing the matter of the Queen of Scots's death in her mind, whether it were better to rid her out of the way, or else to spare her, and many great reasons offered themselves on both sides, so as long held in suspense, she would oftentimes sit speechless and her

---

[271] Commonplace author omits 'which some deemed not only inhumane, but tyrannical and heathenish'.

[272] 'small' in the original.

[273] 'Queen Elizabeth's' in the original.

[274] Baker, p. 271 (jumps to a new section in the original).

countenance cast down; at last her feel prevailing she delivered to secretary Davison letters under her hand and seal, to get the Commission made under the great Seal of England for the execution of the Queen of Scots, which might be in a readiness upon any fear of danger, charging him, not to disclose the matter to any whomsoever. But the next day her mind was altered, and sent Sir William Killigrew to countermand the making of the Commission; whereupon Davison goes to the Queen and lets her know that the Commission was already made, and the Seal put to it, where at the Queen extremely angry rebuked him sharply for his hastiness, yet Davison imparted the matter to the Privy Councellors and persuades them that the Queen commanded the Commission should be put in execution. Hereupon the Clerk of the Council Mr Beale is sent down with letters wherein authority is deputed to the Earls of Kent, Shrewsbury, Derby, Cumberland and others that she should be put to death according to Law; with which proceeding the Queen was not once made acquainted; and more than this; although she had intimated to Davison, that she would take some other order concerning the Queen of Scots, yet did he not stay Beale from going.

And now comes the last act of the Queen of Scots' tragedy; for as soon as the Earls were come to Fotheringay, they together with Sir Amias Pawlet, and Sir Drue Drury, with whom she was in custody go unto her and reading the Commission, signify the cause of their coming: and in a few words admonish her to prepare herself for death, for that she must die the next day. Whereto without any change of countenance or passion of mind, she made answer; I had not thought that my sister the Queen would have consented to my death who am not subject to your laws: but since it is her pleasure, death shall then be most welcome to me. Then she requested that she might confer with her Confessor and Melvin her steward, which would not be granted; the Bishop or Dean of Peterborough they offered her but them she refused. The Lords being gone from her, she gave order that supper should be hastened where she eat (as she used to do) soberly and sparingly; and perceiving her men and women servants to weep and lament, she comforted them and bid them rejoice at her that she was now to depart out of a world of misery. After supper, she looked over her will, read the inventory of her goods and jewels and writ there names severally by them, to whom she gave any of them; at her wonted hour she went to bed, and after a few hours sleep, awaking, she spent the rest of the night at her devotion.

And now the fatal day being come, which was the 8th of February she gets up[275] and made her ready in her best apparel, and then betook her self into her closet, to Almighty God, imploring his assistance with deep sighs and groans, until Thomas Andrews Sheriff of the County gave notice, that it was time to come forth, and then with a princely majesty and a cheerful countenance she came out her head covered with a linen veil, and carrying an ivory crucifix in her hand; in the gallery the Earls met her and the other Gentlemen, Mr Melvin her servant, upon his bended knees deplored his own fortune that he should be the messenger to

---

[275] Now the commonplace author is imitating the original's use of the historical present tense, this exciting description of the execution conveying a sense of immediacy.

carry this sad news into Scotland, when the Queen comforted saying, do not lament Melvin, thou shalt by and by see Mary Steward freed from all cares; then turning herself to the Earls she requested that her servants might stand by her at her death, which the Earl of Kent was very loath to grant for fear of superstition.[276] To which she said fear nothing my Lord, these poor wretches desire only to give me my last farewell. I know the Queen my sister would not deny me so small a request; after this the Earls and the Sheriff of the County leading the way, she came to the scaffold, which was placed at the upper end of the hall, where was a chair, a cushion, and a block, all covered with mourning; then the Dean of Peterborough going to prayers she falling upon her knees, and holding up the crucifix in both her hands, prayed with her servants in Latin out of the Office of the Blessed Virgin. Prayers being ended, she kissed the crucifix and signing herself with the sign of the cross said 'as thy arms, O Christ, were forced[277] forth upon the cross, so embrace me with the open arms of thy mercy and forgive me my sins'. The executioner then asking her pardon, she forgave him; and now her women helping off her outer garments and breaking forth into shrieks and cries, she kissed them, signed them with the cross, and willed them to leave lamenting, for now an end of her sorrows was at hand; and then shadowing her face with a linen cloth and lying down on the block, she repeated the Psalm, In te Domine speravi, ne confundar in

---

[276] Meaning that he feared they would collect relics from her execution that would lead to her being worshipped as a saint.

[277] 'spread' in the original.

aeternum;[278] at which words, she stretching forth her body, her head was at 2 blows taken off. Her body was afterward royally buried in the Cathedral Church at Peterborough; but since that her noble son King James King of Great Britain erected a royal monument for her in King Henry VII chapel at Westminster.

This sad tragic[279] end had Mary Steward Queen of Scots in the 46th year of her age; a lady so complete in all excellent parts of body and mind, that must needs have made her a happy woman, if she had not been a Queen; and perhaps a happy Queen too if she had not been heir to the crown of England for why did all her endeavours want success, but only from the fear of the succession; and no innocence of hers could be a defence, where the fury of jealousy made the assault.

[280]In the 15th year of Queen Elizabeth's reign, Thomas Howard Duke of Norfolk on the 16th day of January, was brought to his trial in Westminster Hall, where sat as Commissioners George Talbott, Earl of Shrewsbury (made High Steward of England for the day) Reynold Grey, Earl of Kent, Thomas Ratcliff, Earl of Sussex, Henry Herbert Earl of Pembroke, Edward Seymour, Earl of Hertford, Ambrose Dudley, Earl of Warwick, Robert Dudley, Earl of Leicester; Walter Devereux, Viscount Hereford, Edward Clinton Lord Admiral, William Lord Howard of Effingham, Chamberlain; William Cecil, Lord Burleigh, Secretary; Arthur Lord Grey

---

[278] The last two lines of the 'Te Deum' prayer, translated as 'O Lord in thee I have trusted, let me never be confounded'.

[279] Words 'sad, tragic' added by commonplace author.

[280] Baker, p. 250.

of Wilton; James Blount, Lord Mountjoy; William Lord Sands, Thomas Lord Wentworth, William Lord Borough, Lewis Lord Mordant; John Pawlet, Lord St John of Basing; Robert Lord Rich; Roger Lord North; Edmund Bruges, Lord Chandois; Oliver Lord St John of Bletso; Thomas Sackville, Ld Buckhurst and William West, Ld de la Ware. After silence, Sir Owen Houton, Lieutenant of the Tower was[281] commanded to bring the Duke to the Bar and then the Clerk of the Crown said Thomas Duke of Norfolk, late of Keningale in the County of Norfolk, hold up thy hand, which done, the Clerk with a loud voice read the crimes laid to his charge; that in the 11th year of the Queen's reign, he had traitorously consulted to make her away, and to bring in foreign forces for invading the kingdom. Also, that he dealt with the Queen of Scots, concerning marriage, contrary to his promise made to the Queen under his hand writing. Also that he relieved with money, the Earls of Northumberland and Westmorland that had stirred up rebellion against the Queen. Also that in the 13th year of the Queen's reign, he implored auxiliary forces of Pope Pius V, the Queen's professed enemy, of the King of Spain of the Duke D'Avila, for the freeing of the Queen of Scots, and restoring of the Popish Religion; and lastly, that he sent supply to the Lord Harris and other the Queen's enemies in Scotland.

These indictments being read, the Clerk demanded of the Duke, if he were guilty of these crimes or not? Here the Duke requested he might be allowed to have Counsel; but Chief Justice Catline made answer, that it was not lawful; yet (said the Duke) I have heard that Humphrey Stafford, in

---

[281] 'is' in original.

the reign of King Henry VII in a cause of treason had one assigned to plead for him. To which Dyer, Chief Justice of the Common Pleas made reply that Stafford had Counsel assigned him concerning the right of sanctuary, from whence he was taken by force, but in the indictment of treason, he pleaded his own cause. After this the Duke yielding to be tried by his peers, first Barham, Sergeant at Law then Gerrard, the Attorney General[282] and lastly Bromley, the Queen's Solicitor enforced the crimes, objected against him, to all which the Duke made colourable answers but most of them being proved by sufficient testimony, he asked upon occasion, whether the subjects of another Prince who is confederate and in league with the Queen are to be accounted the Queen's enemies. To which Catline answered they were, and that the Queen of England might wage war with any Duke of France and yet hold firm peace with the French King. When it grew towards night, the Lord High Steward demanded of the Duke if he had any more to say for himself; who answered no, I rely upon the equity of the laws.

After this the Lords withdrew a while out of the court,[283] and then returning, the Lord Steward beginning at the lowermost asked them my Lord De La Ware, is Thomas Duke of Norfolk guilty of these crimes of High Treason, for which he is called in question. He rising up, and laying his hand upon his breast, answered guilty, in like manner they answered all. After this, the Lord Steward with tears in his eyes stood

---

[282] 'Queen's Attorney' in the original.

[283] 'out of the court' added by commonplace author.

up and pronounced sentence after the usual form;[284] but though the Duke was now condemned, yet the Queen was so tender of his case, that it was 4 months after before he was executed at last on the 2^d of June at 8 of the clock in the morning, he was brought to the scaffold upon Tower Hill, and there executed.[285]

43.[286] As soon as it came to the knowledge of Queen Elizabeth that the Queen of Scots was put to death, her countenance grew dejected and her speech failed her insomuch that all in her mourning weeds, she gave herself over to sorrow, commanded her Councellors from her presence,[287] and caused Davison to be cited to the Star-Chamber before these delegates, Sir Christopher Wrey, Lord Chief Justice of the King's Bench, for that time made Lord Privy Seal, The Archbishop of Canterbury and York, the Earls of Worcester, Cumberland, and Lincoln, The Lords Grey and Lumley, Sir James Croft, Comptroller of the Queen's House, Sir Walter Mildmay, Chancellor of the Exchequer; Sir Edmund Anderson, Lord Chief Justice of the Common Pleas, and Sir Roger Manwood; (where note that Bromley Lord Chancelor, Burleigh Lord Treasurer, the Earl of Leicester, and Sir Christopher Hatton, who were indeed

---

[284] Commonplace author omits short discussion of the fate of two accomplices of the Duke of Norfolk who were also executed.

[285] 'Beheaded' in the original.

[286] Baker, pp. 271-2.

[287] The commonplace author omits section about a letter written by Elizabeth to King James denying responsibility for Mary's death and desiring what was best for him.

more guilty of the fact than Davison, were none of the number). Before these delegates, Popham the Queen's Attorney, lays to Davison's charge, contempt of the Queen's Majesty violation of his trust, and neglect of his duty laying open all the particulars of his fact; which afterward Egerton, the Queen's Solicitor, Gawdy and Puckering her Sergeants at Law urged also against him with great aggravation. To which Davison mildly answered that he would not contest with the Queen only presents that if he had done any thing otherwise than he ought, it was out of ignorance and mistaking; and not out of any purpose to disobey her Majesty. It seems the Queen had carried herself as one that would have it done, and yet was loath to do it, scarce knowing her own mind, and yet would have another know it; meaning to make it the work of mistaking, rather than of purpose; that so at least she might leave some place of satisfaction to herself, that it was not absolutely of her doing. The pleadings being ended, the Commissioners went to censure, Manwood began and gave his opinion, that Davison for the inconsiderateness of his tact, should be fined 20000 pounds and imprisoned during the Queen's pleasure; the rest went on in that sentence, only the Lord Grey excused Davison so far, that he thought him worthy of reward, rather than of punishment; the conclusion was, that the first sentence for his fine and imprisonment was by Wray, Keeper of the Privy Seal confirmed; and Davison never after recovered the Queen's favour, though she relieved him sometimes in his necessity: He was a man ingenious indeed, but was not very thoroughly acquainted with the ways of the Court, and was thought to have been raised to the place of Secretary, of purpose to act this part and for nothing else.

And the Queen upon the King of Scots calling home his ambassador and thought of nothing but revenge for his mother's death, still laying the fault upon Davison and the unadvised credulity of her councellors by little and little allayed his passion.[288] And to the end, that he should assure himself that the Queen his mother was put to death with out her privity, she sent him this sentence against Davison, under the hand and seals of all the delegates, and attested under the Grand Seal of England; and for the King's further satisfaction, the Queen sent him another instrument signed likewise with the hands of all the judges of England, in which they aver, that the sentence against the Queen of Scots, could in no wise prejudice his right in the succession.

44.[289] In the year 1417, Otto Colonna being newly chosen Pope, by the name of Martin V fell out an accident, which showed strict observance of ecclesiastical censures in those days, which was this. The wives of the Lord Strange, and Sir John Trussel of Warmington in Cheshire, striving for a place at a sermon in St Dunstan's Church in the East in London, their husbands being both present, fell themselves to striving in their wives behalf, insomuch that the quarrel between them grew hot[290] and great part-taking there was of each other's friends and followers at the time, with them many swords were drawn, and in the encounter, some were slain

---

[288] Commonplace author omits section about Elizabeth warning James that he could not expect help from Spain or France if he went to war with England but if he remained an ally he would enjoy her love forever.

[289] Baker, p. 127.

[290] 'grew hot' was added by the commonplace author.

and many wounded, and the disturbance was not a little both in the Church and the adjoining street; the delinquents were thereupon apprehended, and committed to the counter, and the Church was suspended, because of blood shed therein. And upon examination, the Lord Strange being found guilty, as having been the first aggressor,[291] was, by the Archbishop of Canterbury adjudged to do this penance, which was accordingly performed. The Parson of St Dunstan's went before, after whom was followed all the Lords Servants and others that sided with him in this affray, in their shirts; after them followed Lord Strange himself, bare-headed, with a large wax taper in his hand; then followed the Lady, barefooted; and last of all came Reginald Renwood, the Arch-Deacon in which processional order they went from the Cathedral Church of St Paul's, (where the sentence was given) to St Dunstan's Church where at the re-consecration and hallowing thereof the Lady filled all the vessels with water with her own hands fetching it also from the next conduit. And furthermore, according to the Sentence, offered to the altar, an ornament for the same, of the value of 10 pounds and the Lord Pix of Silver of 5 pounds value. This penance, the Lord and Lady would without doubt have gladly redeemed with a great sum of money, if the stricter discipline of the Church had in those days allowed it (for this was in the beginning of King Henry V's time) but it seems, the corrupt use[292] of commutation of Penance, was not as yet come in use.

---

[291] 'as having been the first aggressor' was added by the commonplace author.

[292] 'corrupt use' added by commonplace author.

45. In the year of our Lord 1596 and in the 39th year of the reign of Queen Elizabeth, when Thomas Arundel of Warder in the County of [....][293] returned into England, from the wars in Hungary against the Turk, under the Emperor Rodolphus II [294] to whom for his great services performed in those Wars the Emperor by his Letters Patents created an Earl of the Sacred Empire, all and singular his heir and their posterity, males or females, lawfully descended from him, to be Earls and Countesses of the Holy Empire for ever. Those persons who are graced and dignified [295] with this honourable title, have a place and voice in the Imperial Diets or Parliaments. They may also purchase lands, in any of the Emperor's dominions, they may lead voluntary soldiers; and are not bound to answer any matter, before any Judge, but only in the Imperial Chamber. At this Gentleman's return thus honoured out of Germany, a great question was started, and came in agitation, whether titles of honour given to the Queen's subjects by any foreign Prince without her privity, ought to be accepted by them, or admitted by her. For this new Earl stuck much in the stomachs of the English barons who regretted and inwardly grudged to give him place or presidency before them. The matter was long disputed on both sides, but what issue it had, or whether he were

---

[293] In the original no county name was given. Perhaps the commonplace author checked other books to find a reference to the place named 'Warder' but was unable to do so or he may have forgotten to return to fill in the blank. Thomas Arundel's family originate in Wardour, Wiltshire.

[294] The name of the emperor not given in the original.

[295] 'and dignified' added by commonplace author.

permitted this honour here in England is not made manifest in story or otherwise. Certain it is that Sir Nicholas Clifford, and Sir Anthony Shirley, whom the French King Henry IV two years before, received into the Order of St Michael, were laid in prison at their coming home, and charged to resign their robes and other ensigns of the order.

[4]6.[296] King Henry VIII had 6 wives; his first wife was Katherine, daughter of Ferdinand King of Spain, the relict of his brother Arthur; she lived his wife above 20 years, and was divorced from him; after which she lived 3 years by the name of Katherine Dowager; she deceased at Kimbolton, in the County of Huntington, January 8th 1535 and lies interred in the Cathedral Church of Peterborough, under a hearse of black say, having a white cross in the midst. He had by this wife, Henry, born at Richmond, who lived not full 2 months, and was buried at Westminster also another son, whose name is not mentioned, and lived but a short time neither; then a daughter named Mary, born at Greenwich, in the 8th year of his reign, and came afterward to be Queen of England.

His 2nd wife was Anne, the 2nd daughter of Sir Thomas Bullen, Earl of Wiltshire, and Ormond; she was married to him January 25th 1533, lived his wife 3 years and 4 months, and then was beheaded, and her body buried in the quire of the chapel in the Tower; by this wife he had a daughter named Elizabeth, born at Greenwich, in the 25th year of his reign, who exceeded her sister Mary in years of reign, who

---

[296] Baker, p. 215.

succeeded her sister Mary in the crown. He had also a son by her, but born dead.

His 3rd wife was Jane, daughter of Sir John Seymour, and sister to the Lord Edward Seymour, Earl of Hartford and Duke of Somerset; she was married to him the very next day after the beheading of Queen Anne, lived his wife one year, and 5 months, and then died in childbed, and was buried in the midst of the quire of the church within the castle of Windsor; by this wife he had a son, named Edward, born at Hampton Court, in the 29th year of his reign, who succeeded him in the kingdom.

His 4th wife was Anne, sister to the Duke of Cleve, she lived his wife 6 months only, and was divorced. She remained in England long after the King's death, and accompanied the Lady Elizabeth through London, at the solemnizing of Queen Mary's coronation. Of this lady, this passage is related; that when her ladies, one time said unto her, that they looked now every day to hear of her great belly, she answered they might look long enough, unless saying 'how dost though sweetest; good morrow sweet heart', and such like words, could make a great belly, for said she more than this never passed between the King and me. She died in the 4th year of Queen Mary, and was buried at Westminster

His 5th wife was Katherine, daughter of Edmond, and niece of Thomas Howard, his brother, Duke of Norfolk. She was married to him in the 32 year of his reign and lived his wife 1 year and a half, and then was beheaded in the Tower of London for incontinency, and buried in the chancel of the chapel near Queen Ann Bollen.

His 6th wife was Katherine, daughter of Sir Thomas Parre of Kendall, and sister to the Lord William Parre, Marquess of Northampton; she was the relict of John Nevil, Lord Latimer, and was married to King Henry at Hampton Court in the 35th year of his reign; she was his wife 3 years, and 6 months; and then surviving him, was again married to Sir Thomas Seymour, Lord Admiral of England unto whom she bore a daughter, but died in childbed, anno 1548.

This King had many mistresses besides these many wives, which he affected and kept privately in several places to whom he privately resorted, by whom it is probable he might have had divers children, yet it is nowhere mentioned that [..]er any was owned by him, save only one and that was a son named Henry Fitz-Roy, begotten on the body of the Lady Tabboise, called Elizabeth Blunt, born at Blackamore in Essex, in the 20th year of his reign, whom he created Duke of Richmond and Somerset, who married Mary, daughter of Thomas Howard Duke of Norfolk, with whom he lived not long, but died at St James's, and was buried at Framlingham in Suffolk.

[4.]7[297] Edward III created the County of Lancaster to be a County Palatine, and honoured the Duke of Lancaster there with giving him Jura Regalia, having a particular court. The Officers whereof, were the Chancellor, the Attorney, the Receiver General, the Clerk of the Court, the auditors, the surveyors and the messenger. The Seal of the Duchy of Lancaster remains always with the Chancellor; but the Seal

---

[297] Baker, p. 118.

of the County Palatine remains in a chest always in the County Palatine, under the trust and safe custody of a Keeper. Now all grants, and leases of lands, tenements and offices in the County Palatine of Lancaster, should pass under that Seal, and no other; but all grants and leases out of the County Palatine, and within the survey of the Duchy, should pass under the Seal of the Duchy, and no other. Otherwise such grants are void, ipso facto. Though this County Palatine was a younger brother, yet it had more honours, manors, lordships and lands annexed unto it, than any of the rest, and all by Acts of Parliament whereby [...]d the franchises, privileges, immunities, and freedoms, which the Duke of Lancaster had for himself, his men and tenants, were confirmed. All which prerogatives and enfranchisements of the said Duchy of Lancaster, King Henry IV by his royal charter, and concurrence of Parliament granted and ratified; and did also sever the possessions of the said Duchy from the crown. Which separation was made by the said Henry IV in regard he well knew that he had the Duchy of Lancaster (Par Regno) by a sure and indefeasible title, where as his title to the crown was not so assured; because that after the death of King Richard II the royal right was in the heir of Lionel, Duke of Clarence, the 2nd son of King Edward III and John of Gaunt, who was father to Henry IV was the 4th son of Edward III. Therefore his policy was, to make a Duchy a distinct thing from the Crown, for fear of after-claps [...] liberty of the Duchy, was used to be governed by the Chancellor, who had under him a Steward, that kept Court Leet with an Attorney of the Duchy; there were also 4 burgesses, and 4 assistants, a bayliff, who had others under him. 5 constables, 4 wardens, that kept the stock for the poor, four wardens for the highways, a jury of 14 ale combers who looked to the well brewing of ale, and to the assize of all measures wet and dry, 4 scavengers, and a beadle and the common prison for all great offences committed within the liberty of the Duchy in Newgate.[298] This liberty [...] established to perpetuity by the statutes of King Edward IV and King Henry VII pertaining to the Duchy of Lancaster begins without Temple-Bar westward on the north side of the Thames, and stretches west to Ivy-bridge where it terminates, and again on the north side that middle row or troop of small tenements without Temple-Bar, partly opening to the south and partly towards the north, up west to a stone cross over against the Strand, and this is the bounds of the said liberty, which first belonged to Brian Lille, or de Insula, after to Peter of Savoy, and then to the House of Lancaster.

48.[299] King Henry the 3rd did grant to his Uncle Peter of Savoy, all those houses at that time situated upon the Thames, which appertained to one Brian Lisle or de Insula, in the way or the street, called the Strand, to hold to him and his heirs. Yielding three gilded arrows every year in the Exchequer this Peter, Earl of Savoy and Richmond, was son to Thomas Earl of Savoy, brother to Boniface, Archbishop of Canterbury and uncle unto Eleanor, wife to the said King

---

[298] James Howell, *Londinopolis* (London, 1657) p. 93. Starting reading from a new book without making notes in a new paragraph only happens here.

[299] It is not clear why this is a new numbered paragraph. Normally that indicates a new book being used, or a different section of the same book, but here the copied text simply runs on in the original.

Henry III and was the first founder of the Savoy anno 1245 which he gave afterward to the fraternity of Mountjoy. But then Queen Eleanor did purchase it for Edmund, Duke of Lancaster her son, of the same Brotherhood,[300] which Duke did much augment and improve the structure. John the French King, who was taken prisoner at the battle of Poiters[301] by Edward the Black Prince, was lodged there, being then the fairest manor house of England.

About 30 years after, anno 1381, the rebels of Kent and Essex did most barbarously burn this Princely house, with many goodly vessels of gold and silver which they found then hurling them all into the Thames, all which they did out of a popular malice to John of Gaunt, Duke of Lancaster, in whose possession it then was in right of his wife [blank space] the only daughter of the aforesaid Edmund.[302] It came afterward to the King's hands, and King Henry VII did re-edify and raise it up again, but converted it to the Hospital of St John Baptist, yet was he content, that it should still be called the Savoy, and bestowed lands for the maintenance of 100 poor men; but afterwards it was suppressed by his grandchild King Edward VI, the beds and bedding, with other furniture, were given to the City of London; together with the palace of Bridewell, to be a work-house, and house of correction for idle persons and some of the Savoy furniture was given also to furnish St Thomas Hospital in

---

[300] 'fraternity' in original.

[301] This detail about the battle of Poitiers was added by the commonplace author.

[302] This detail about John of Gaunt's wife was added by the commonplace author. This is another example of the author leaving a blank space, intending to return to the manuscript later to fill it in.

Southwark. But afterwards the Savoy Hospital was re-founded, and endowed with lands by Queen Mary, who made one Jackson first master thereof, and it is memorable, how the Queen's maids of honour, and the ladies of the court, in those times did largely contribute for storing it again with new beds, and all other necessary furniture; and so it hath continued ever since. The chapel of this hospital serves now for a parish church to the neighbours near adjoining thereunto, and for others.

49.[303] Henry Garnet, Superior of the Jesuits in England was tried at Guildhall in the city of London on Friday, Mar 28th 1606 for having a hand in the Gunpowder Treason, and being found guilty by the Jury, and judgment pronounced against him to be drawn, hanged and quartered; he was accordingly executed May the 3rd following, upon a scaffold set up for that purpose at the west end of St Paul's Church and the passages at his execution were as follows:

At his ascending to the Scaffold, he stood much amazed (fear and guilt appearing in his face) the Deans of St Paul's and Winchester being present very gravely and Christianly exhorted him to a true and lively faith to God-ward, and a free and plain acknowledgment of his offence; and if any further treason lay in his knowledge to unburden his

---

[303] Taken from James I's *The Gunpowder Treason* (London, 1679), pp. 147-148. This book was based on a proclamation issued by James in 1605 entitled *His Majesties Speech in the Last Session of Parliament* (London, 1605), also known as the 'King's Book'. However, this extract must be derived from the later 1679 version because it describes Henry Garnet's execution, which took place in May 1606, after the publications of James's initial proclamation.

conscience; and show a sorry and detestation of it. But Garnet impatient of persuasions, and ill pleased to be exhorted by them desired them not to trouble him; he came prepared and was resolved. Then the Recorder of London (who was by his Majesty appointed to be there) asked Garnet if he had anything to say unto the people before he died; it was no time to dissemble, and now his treasons were too manifest to be dissembled; therefore if he would, the world should witness, what at last he censured of himself, and of his fact, it should be free for him to speak what he listed. But Garnet unwilling to take the offer, said his voice was low, his strength gone, and the people could not hear him, though he spoke to them. But to those about him on the scaffold, he said, the intention was wicked, and the fact would have been cruel, and from his soul he would have abhorred it, had it effected; but he said, he only had general knowledge of it by Mr Catesby, which in that he disclosed it not, nor used means to prevent it, herein he had offended; what he knew in particular was in his confession, as he said, but the Recorder wished him to be remembered, that the King's Majesty had under his own handwriting these 4 points amongst others

1. That Greenway told him of this, not as a fault, but as a thing which he had intelligence of, and told it him by way of consultation

2. That Catesby and Greenway came to him to be absolved

3. That Mr Tesmond and he had a conference of the particulars of the Powder-Treason in Essex long after.

4. That Greenway had asked him, who should be the Protector? But Garnet said, that was to be referred till the blow was past.

These prove your privity, said the Recorder, and these are extant under your hand, Garnet answered whatsoever was under his hand was true. And for that he disclosed not to his Majesty the things he knew, he confessed himself justly condemned. And for this did ask forgiveness of his Majesty. Hereupon the Recorder led him to the side of the scaffold, to make his confession public. Then Garnet said, good countrymen, I am come hither this blessed day; of the invention of the holy cross, to end all my crosses in this life. The cause of my suffering is not unknown to you, I confess I have offended the King and am sorry for it, so far as I was guilty, which was in concealing it, and for that I ask pardon of his Majesty. This treason intended against the King[304] was bloody; my self should have detested it, had it taken effect; and I am heartily sorry that any Catholics ever had so cruel a design. Then turning himself from the people to them about him he made an apology for Mrs Anne Vaux, saying there is such an Honourable Gentlewoman, who hath been[305] very much wronged in report, for it is suspected, and said, that I should be married to her or worse; but I protest the contrary, she is a virtuous Gentlewoman, and for me a perfect pure virgin; and for the Pope's breves,[306] Sir Edmund Barnames

---

[304] In the original 'and state'.

[305] Again 'been' in the original, 'bin' in the commonplace book.

[306] i.e. writ or edict.

going overseas and the matter of the Powder-Treason, he referred himself to his arraignment and his confessions, for said he, whatsoever is under my hand in any of my confessions, is true.

Then addressing himself to execution he kneeled at the foot of the ladder, and asked if he might have time to pray, and how long? It was answered he should limit himself; none should interrupt him; it appeared he could not devoutly or constantly pray; fear of death; or hope of pardon, even then so distracted him for often in those prayers he would break off, turn and look about him, and answer to what he overheard, while he seemed to be praying. When he stood up, the Recorder finding in his behaviour as it were an expectation of a pardon wished him not to deceive himself, nor beguile his own soul, he was come to die, and must die requiring him not to equivocate with his last breath. If he knew any thing that might be dangerous to the King or state he should now utter it. Garnet said it is no time now to equivocate, how it was lawful, and when he had showed his mind elsewhere. But said he, I do not now equivocate, and more than I have confessed I do not know.

At his ascending up the ladder, he desired to have warning before he was turned off. But it was told him he must look for no other turn but death. Being upon the gibbet, he used these words, I commend me to all good Catholics, and I pray God preserve his Majesty the Queen and all the posterity, and my Lords of the Privy Council, to whom I remember my humble duty, and I am sorry that I did dissemble with them. But I did not think they had had such proof against me, till it was showed me; But when that was proved, I held it more honour for me at that time to confess, than before to have accused. And for my brother Greenway I would the truth were known for the false reports that are make him more guilty[307] than he is.[308] I pray God the Catholics may not fare the worse for my sake, and I exhort them all they take heed, they enter not into any treasons, rebellions or insurrections against the King and with this he ended speaking and fell to praying and crossing himself said, In nomine Patris et Filii et Spiritus Sancti, and prayed Maria mater gratiae, Maria mater misericordia, tu me a malo protégé et hora mortis susipe; Then in manus tuas Domine, commendo spiritum meum, Then pace tuam in corde meo Domine. Let me always remember the cross, and so returned again to Maria mater gratiae, and then was turned off, and hung till he was dead.[309]

50.[310] The title of the Earl of Richmond to the Crown of England after the death of Richard III slain at Bosworth Field,[311] whereupon he was immediately proclaimed King of England, by the name of Henry VII (setting aside the saying of Philip the Hardy, King of France, that Kingdoms only

---

[307] 'faulty' in the original.

[308] Commonplace author omits a statement saying that Garnet only accused Greenway because he thought he was safe.

[309] Latin translates as 'In the name of the father, son and holy spirit'; 'Mother Mary, give me your mercy, protect me at the hour of my death'; 'in your hands Lord, I commend my spirit'; 'give me peace in my heart, Lord'; 'Mary mother of grace'.

[310] Nathaniel Bacon: *A Continuation of a Historicall Discourse* (London, 1651), pp. 111-112. There is a later edition (1689) but the transcription of this passage is identical to the 1651 original.

[311] Added by commonplace author as contextual information.

belong to them that can get them)[312] would hardly endure the touch, till Pope Innocent VIII by his Bull confirmed the crown to him to hold by a 6 fold Right; 1. of inheritance; 2. of war; 3. of espousals; 4. of election; 5. of gift by parliament; and 6. of pontifical benediction which the King liked very well, and the rather because his title by marriage was buried up in the middle and so made the less noise. For though it was his best guard, yet he liked not that it should be so reputed, lest his title should seem rather conferred on him, than gained by him; and so should hold by a woman, or at the best by the curtsy of England. If the people's favour should so far extend the law in that point, by both which he holds the honour of a complete English King diminished. His title by inheritance is much disputable, if the right heirs of John of Gaunt be inquired after. And much more that title by the sword,[313] for although that invested him in the possession, yet gave it no right or title, but by wrong which may indeed be plastered over by election, or by an Act of Parliament but then he must become tenant to the people. As touching the pontifical benediction, himself took that but as a redundancy, that might sway with the clergy and do his title no hurt. Nevertheless, what these cannot as severally, by joint concurrences he accounts so fully done, as if he were a King against all the world,[314] and more. Yet he is not sure enough; but, as one jealous, is more watchful; [315] so his eye is upon his title. There is his guard, and regard, as if it were

---

[312] Omits reference included by Bacon: Thevet. lib. 4. cap. 32.

[313] 'by war' in the original.

[314] Omits a classical reference included by Bacon: Jovius Brit.

[315] 'tender' in the original.

the out-works of his crown; which once lost, the crown cannot hold but long. In this he minded so much his grandeur[316] that he lost the repute of his candour;[317] then casting his eye up to the government, and finding it of a mixed temper, wherein if royalty prevails not, popularity will. Therefore like a good soldier, while his strength is full, he briskly sallies upon the people's liberties, in regard of their persons, which such cunning[318] as he taught the people to dance more often and better to the tune of prerogative and allegiance, than all his predecessors had done. Nor did the people perceive it, till it was too late,[319] and then they saw their condition such as that it was in vain for them to wrangle with their own Acts. So that having thus gained the allegiance of the persons of the people; their estates more easily followed; and therefore, though in the former he wrought of Ambuscade,[320] in this he may be more brave and charge them in the front;[321] which yet he did also by such cunning gradations,[322] that he accomplished his ends; and thus serving his prerogative with power and his purse with

---

[316] 'greatness' in the original.

[317] 'goodness' in the original. Bacon rhymes 'greatness' and 'goodness', while our commonplace author rhymes 'grandeur' with 'candour'.

[318] 'cunning conveyance' in the original.

[319] 'till they were over their shoes' in the original.

[320] i.e. an ambush.

[321] 'in the Van' in the original.

[322] 'degrees' in original.

his prerogative, he made all serve his own turn, and so settled himself absolutely in the throne.[323]

51.[324] When Queen Mary married, she aimed not only at a foreign blood, but at a Prince in Majesty and power exceeding her own, and thereby seeking advancement both to herself and her realm, endangered both. The matter was long in debate between the Spanish and English, and at length after they had busied their wits[325] on either side; a supremacy is formed, suitable to the Lord and husband of Queen Mary, that could not be content to be one inch lower than herself. Philip had the name of a King, and precedence and in some cases not without the allegiance of the English. Their offences against his person equally treason, with those against his own person and indictments run, Contra Pacem et Coronam D. Regis et Regine.[326] That in some cases he participated in the regal power may appear;[327] in the Articles he was to aid the Queen in the administration of the Kingdom. He joined with the Queen in the royal assent to bills, and in Commissions, letters patents, and in writs of summons of Parliament as well as others, that in the words,

---

[323] Commonplace author omits short description of how Henry VII abused his prerogative and reference given in original: Jovius Brit. fol. 9.Humanitatem omnem vincente periculo.

[324] Bacon, p. 164 (or page 154 in the 1651 edition).

[325] 'about ten years' in the original. Plus reference to Sleiden missing in the commonplace version.

[326] 'against the peace and person of God's King and Queen'.

[327] Reference given in original omitted here 1 Ph. and Mar. Parl. 2. cap. 1.

the crown is referred only to the Queen. Now if the King had broken this agreement either the Parliament must over-rule the whole, or all that is done must be undone, and England must bear the burden; so that doubtless a Queen Regent is a dangerous condition for England,[328] unless she be married only to the people.

This was observed by Queen Elizabeth who therefore kept herself unmarried, nor did the people otherwise desire her marriage than in relation to posterity. Few of them liking any one of their own nation so well as to prefer him so highly above themselves, and fewer any foreigner. This was soon espied by foreign Princes and the lady her self perceiving that she was like to receive prejudice hereby, in her interest among them signified by her Ambassadors that she never made to stoop so low as to match with any of her subjects, but intended to make her choice from some foreign Prince who neither by power or riches should be able to prejudice the interest of any of her neighbouring Princes. A very pretty complement this was to gain expectation from those abroad, and a better correspondence thereunto. Upon this ground, divers Princes conceived hopes of more interest, than by trial they could find. And the Arch-duke of Austria began a treaty, which seemingly was entertained by her, but her proposals were such, as silenced all those of the Austrian interest for ever after, viz:

1. That the Romish religion should never be admitted into England

---

[328] 'above that of an infant king' omitted.

2. That no man that she married should ever wear the title of King

3. That no foreigner should even intermeddle in the rule and government of the Church or Commonwealth, nor in the ministry of the Church

4. That is he should marry and survived the Queen, he should never challenge any title or interest in the government or any possession in England.

5. That she would never marry any one, she might not first see.

So as it seemed she aimed at some inferior Prince that durst not look so high or else that she did but make semblance, till she was nigh 40 years old after which all pretensions of that kind would cease. And in all declared, that she liked not her sister Mary's choice[329] and so to the grief of her people died without issue of her body.

52.[330] The English throne hath often been possessed by such Kings as could not boast much of their birth-right, yet so loved the title thereto by that of inheritance as it made them strain their pedigree hard to make both ends meet, and to bring themselves within the Degrees. Of 23 Kings from the Saxons' time to King James,[331] 4 of the first Norman Princes

---

[329] In the original, the section ends here. So commonplace author added 'to the grief of her people'.

[330] Bacon (1651), pp. 152-153.

[331] 'to king James' added in commonplace book.

had no title by inheritance viz William I William II, Henry I and King Stephen. Henry II and Richard I had right of birth, yet came in by compact. The 7th which was King John, had no title but election. The 8th was Henry III came in a child, and contrary to compact between the nobility, and Prince Lewis of France. The 9th and 10th were Edward I and Edward II, these succeeded as by unquestionable title of descent, yet the nobles were pre-engaged. The 11th was Edward III in his entry eldest son but not heir for his father was alive; 'tis true there were other children of Edward III alive that were more worthy of the crown, but they were too many to agree in any but a child, that might be ruled by themselves, and so submitted to Richard II heir to Edward III the 12th number. The 3 next ensuing Kings were of the collateral line, Henry IV, Henry V and Henry VI and were the 13th 14th and 15th. Their 2 successors Edward IV and Edward V were of the right line; yet Edward IV came in by Disseisin and Edward V by permission, these were in number the 16th and 17th. Then the 18 and 19th were Richard III and Henry VII who were collateral to one another and to the right blood. The 20th was Henry VIII though when he was King he might claim from his mother yet he came in as heir to his father. And if Edward VI was right heir to the house of York by his grandmother and the 21th yet cannot the crown be said to descend upon his 2 sisters Mary and Elizabeth, neither as heirs to him nor to Henry VIII nor to one another, so long as the Statute of their Illegitimation remained[332], which as touching Queen Mary the 22th in order, was till 3 months after her entry upon the throne, and

---

[332] Reference omitted by commonplace author: 28 H. 8. ca. 7. 1 Mar. Sess. 2. cap. 1

as touching Queen Elizabeth for ever, who was the 23th and the last. For that virago provided for herself by way of repeal of the said Act of Illegitimation[333] (as her sister had done) but more tenderly regarding the honour of her father and the Parliament than to mention their blemishes in Government by doing and undoing. She over-looked that Act of Henry VIII and the notion of inheritance, and contented herself with her title with the statute made by her father in his 35th year,[334] which to her was a mere purchase, and was not ashamed to declare to all the world that she did have and hold thereby, and that it was High Treason for any subject to deny that the course of the crown of England is to be ordered by Act of Parliament.[335] And this power did the Parliament exercise, not only in the course of the crown to Queen Mary and Queen Elizabeth but during reign of Queen Elizabeth so far as to disinherit and disable any person who should pretend right to the crown, in opposition to the right of Queen Elizabeth, and upon this point only did the whole proceedings against Mary Queen of Scots depend, who claimed to be,[336] and doubtless was, heir unto Henry VIII after the determination of his right line and yet she was put to death for pretending right by the common law in opposition of the Act of Parliament[337] and this much of the titles of the English Kings since the entrance of the Normans.

---

[333] Added for clarification 'the said Act of Illegitimation'.

[334] Reference omitted: 35 H. 8. cap.

[335] Reference omitted: 13 Eliz. ca. 1.

[336] Reference omitted: Thuan. vol. 1. lib. 20.

[337] This last sentence added by commonplace author.

53.[338] This crown that may be worn by an infant as Edward 6th held it forth, being the 7th President of infancy, ruling under Protectorship since the Norman times[339] may much rather be worn by a woman, whose natural endowments do far exceed the other, and are not inferior unto the most of men. Two examples of this the English Nation have had in the proceeding century,[340] Queen Mary and Queen Elizabeth of several persuasions[341] in matters of religion and liable to exceptions in regard of their sex, by men of the counter-persuasion on both sides; yet both upheld the honour of the English crown, though therein the one more especially being neither engaged in the Roman cause, nor in the estate of marriage as the other was. This was Queen Elizabeth in person a woman but in mind endowed with all the perfections of a man and being invested with the supreme power, she could not endure though a woman to abate one hair[342] of her state and yet upon the sole regard of her sex, she submitted the title of supremacy to a more moderate name of Supreme Governor whereas her father would be called Supreme Head as if it were not only hazardous but hideous for a woman to be Supreme Head of the Church[343] and for this cause would she not revive the statute which her

---

[338] Bacon (1651), pp. 148-149.

[339] Large section of the original omitted here comprising a detailed discussion of the royal prerogative.

[340] In the original 'we have two examples in these times'.

[341] 'Professions' in original.

[342] 'one hair's breadth' in the original

[343] Reference omitted: 26 H. 8. cap. 1.

father made, her brother Edward VI continued and her sister Queen Mary repealed.[344] Nevertheless such as she was, she had all jurisdictions, privileges, superiorities and preminences, spiritual and ecclesiastical, as by any ecclesiastical power and authority formerly had been[345], or might be lawfully exercised, for visitation of the ecclesiastical state and persons and for reformation, order and correction of the same and of all manner of errors, heresies, schisms, abuses, offences, contempt and enormities. She had therefore neither absolute empire, nor absolute jurisdiction over the Churches, neither power to make, declare, alter or repeal any law concerning the same,[346] neither did she ever exercise any such power, but only by Act of Parliament.[347] She had a power over ceremonies in the worship of God, which was given her by the Parliament to execute by advice, and therefore was limited, as also all the remainder of her power in jurisdiction ecclesiastical. For she could do nothing in her own person, but by commission; and these commissioners must be natives and denizens, not foreigners; and the same to be but in certain cases, and with certain process and some cases of ecclesiastical cognisance were referred to trial at the Common Law[348] which were such as concerned the public worship of God, in cases of forfeiture and imprisonment. Lastly, the Queen neither had, nor her Commissioners, nor

---

[344] Reference omitted: 1 Eliz. cap. 1.

[345] 'been' in Bacon, 'bin' in the manuscript.

[346] 'concerning the same' added for clarification.

[347] Reference omitted: 1 Eliz. cap. 3

[348] Reference omitted: 13 El. ca. 12. 23 El. cap. 1.viz.

Bishops, absolute power over the Church censures. No censure was regarded but excommunication, and that no further then the Writ de excommunicato capiendo;[349] and in all cases the same was to be regulated according to the statute in that case provided[350] or by the Common Law in case of action. In all which it is plain, that it is now to be found. That jurisdiction in cases ecclesiastical, was ever absolutely settled in the crown,[351] or claimed and exercised by Queen Elizabeth.

54.[352] In the year 1576 or thereabout; that field of old time called Lolesworth, now Spittle field was broken up[353] to make bricks. In the digging whereof, many earthen pots called 'urnae' were found full of ashes, with burnt bones of men, to wit, of the Romans that inhabited here. For it was the custom of the Ancient Romans to burn their dead, to put their ashes in an urn, and bury the same with certain ceremonies, in some field appointed for that purpose near unto their city and commonly, there was another urn of fresh water set by the other, denoting the tears of their friends.[354] Every of these pots had in them (with the ashes of the dead) one piece of copper money, with the inscription of the

---

[349] Writ ordering the seizing and imprisonment of the excommunicated person until they submit to the will of the Church.

[350] Reference omitted: 5 Eliz. ca. 23

[351] Last clause is added by the commonplace author.

[352] John Stow, *Survey of London* (London, 1598), p. 98.

[353] In original 'for clay'.

[354] This clause about tears of friends does not appear in the original.

Emperor then reigning. Some of them were of Claudius,[355] some of Nero, of Antoninus Pius, of Trajanius and others. Besides those urns, many other pots were found, in the same place, made of a whitish[356] earth, with long necks and handles like[357] stone jugs. These were empty but seemed to be buried full of some liquid matter, long since consumed and soaked through; for there were found divers vials, and other fashioned glasses; some most cunningly wrought,[358] and some of crystal, all which had water in them (which it seems were the tear bottles)[359] nothing differing in cleanness, taste or favour from common spring water, whatsoever it was at first, some of these glasses had oil in them very thick, and earthy in smell; some were supposed to have balm in them but had lost the virtue: many of these pots and glasses were broken in cutting of the clay, so that few were taken up whole.

There were also found divers dishes and cups of a fine red coloured earth, which outwardly showed such a shining smoothness, as if they had been of coral, those had Roman Letters printed in the bottoms; there were also lamps of white and red earth, artificially wrought with divers antiques about them some 3 or 4 images and made of white earth, each of them about a span long; one was of Pallas.[360]

---

[355] 'some of Vespasian' omitted.

[356] 'white' in original.

[357] Original 'like to our stone jugs'. Again, removing personal pronoun.

[358] Original 'such as I have not seen the like'.

[359] This clause in brackets added by commonplace author.

[360] Original 'one I remember was of Pallas, the others I have forgotten'.

Among divers of those antiquities, there was found[361] one urn, with ashes and bones, and one pot of white earth very small, not exceeding the quantity of a quarter of a wine pint, made in shape of a hare squatted upon her legs and between her ears is the mouth of the pot. There hath also been found (in the same field) divers coffins of stone, containing the bones of men. These were supposed to be the burials of some special persons, in the time of the Britons or Saxons after that the Romans had left to govern in Britain.[362] Moreover, there were also found the skulls and bones of men without coffins; or rather whose coffins[363] (being of timber) were consumed; divers great nails of iron were there found, such as are used in the wheels of shod carts; being each one of them as big as a man's finger, and a span[364] long or more their heads being 2 over. Those nails were more wondered at than the rest of the things there found, and many opinions of men were there passed upon them; namely that the men there buried were murdered by driving those nails into their heads.[365] But touching this matter indeed; there were then[366] the bones of a man lying, the head north, the feet south and round about him (athwart his head) along both his sides, and athwart his feet, such nails were found; wherefore it was conjectured, they were the nails of his coffin, which had been a thick bough cut out of some great

---

[361] Original 'I myself have reserved'.

[362] Original 'here'.

[363] Stow, p. 99.

[364] Original 'quarter of a yard'.

[365] Commonplace author omits Stow's scepticism on this explanation.

[366] Original 'I there beheld'.

tree and the same covered with a plank of that thickness, fastened with such nails[367] and found under the broad heads of some of those nails, the old wood was scant turned into earth; but still retaining both the grain and proper colour.

55.[368] Sir William Walworth was a stock-fishmonger, sometime servant to John Lotkin fishmonger and Mayor of London anno 1359 in the time of Edward 3^d.[369] This William Walworth is reported by some to have slain Jack Straw, but Jack Straw being afterward taken was first adjudged by the said Walworth being then Mayor and then beheaded[370] in Smithfield. True it is, that this William Walworth being a man, wise, learned and of incomparable manhood, arrested that presumptuous rebel Wat Tyler upon whom no man durst lay hand, whereby he delivered the King and Kingdom from the barbarous tyranny of wicked traitors. The valiant Mayor arrested him on the head with a sound blow whereupon Tyler furiously struck the Mayor with his dagger; but hurt him not, by reason he was well armed. The Mayor having received his stroke drew his basliard,[371] and grievously wounded Wat in the neck and withall gave him a great blow on the head, in the which conflict, an esquire of the King's house, called John Cavendish drew his sword, and wounded Wat twice or thrice, even to the death, and Wat spurring his

---

[367] Omits 'I caused such nails to be reached up to me'.

[368] James Howell *Londinopolis* (1657), p. 55.

[369] Date added by commonplace author for clarification.

[370] Original 'executed by the loss of his head'.

[371] A small dagger.

horse, cried to the Commons to rescue him, the horse bears him about 30 yards[372] from the place and there he fell down half dead and by and by they which attended on the King encompassed him about, so as he was not seen of his company, many of them thrust him in divers parts of his body and drew him into the Hospital of St Bartholomew from whence again the Mayor caused him to be drawn into Smithfield and there to be beheaded. In reward of his services (the people being dispersed) the King commanded the Mayor to put a basenet on his head, and the Mayor asking, why he should do so, the King answered, he was much bound unto him, and therefore would make him Knight. The Mayor replied that he was neither worthy nor able to take such a dignity[373] upon him, for he was but a merchant, and had to live by his own merchandize only, yet the King made him to put on his basenet, and then with a sword in both his hands he strongly struck him on the neck, as the manner was then and the same day, he made 3 other citizens knights for his sake: viz. John Philpot, Nick Brember, and Robert Kaurd, Aldermen. The Knight gave to the Mayor 100 pounds land by year, and to each of the other 40 pounds land yearly, to their heirs for ever.

[374]It hath also been and is now grown to common opinion, that in reward of this service, by the said William Walworth, against the rebel that King Richard added to the Arms of the City (which was Argent a plain Cross Gules) a Sword or Dagger (for so they term it) whereof a doubt hath been made

---

[372] Original 'eighty foot'.

[373] 'an estate' in the original.

[374] Section from the original omitted on the burial of William Walworth.

by some,[375] and on the contrary alleged that in the 4th year of Richard II in a full assembly in the Upper Chamber in Guildhall, summoned by this William Walworth, then Lord Mayor, as well of Aldermen, as of the Common Council in every word , for certain affairs concerning the King it was by common consent agreed, and ordained, that the old seal of the office of the Mayoralty of the city, being very small, old, unapt and uncomely for the Honour of the city, should be broken and one other new should be had, which the said Mayor commanded to be made artificially and honourably, for the exercise of the said office, thereafter in place of the other. In which new seal, besides the images of St Peter and St Paul which of old were rudely engraved, there should be under the feet of the said images, a shield of the arms of the said city, perfectly graven, with 2 lions supporting the same, and 2 Sergeant at Arms, in the other part, one and 2 tabernacles; in which above, should stand 2 angels, between whom (above the images of Peter and Paul) should be set the Glorious Virgin. This being done, the old seal of the office was delivered to Rich Odiam, Chamberlain, who brake it in pieces, and in place thereof was delivered the new seal to the said Mayor, to use in his Office of Mayoralty, as occasion should require. This new seal seems to be made before William Walworth was knighted for he was not at that time entituled, Sir, as afterwards he was; and certain it is, that the same new seal then made, is now in use, and none other in that Office of the Mayoralty which may suffice to answer the former supposition, without showing any evidence

---

[375] Original 'whereof Mr John Stow made a doubt'.

sealed with the old seal, which was the cross, and sword of St Paul, and not the dagger of William Walworth.

56.[376] The great cross in Cheapside was erected by King Edward 1 anno 1290 upon this occasion. Queen Eleanor his wife died at Hardeby (a town near Lincoln) her body was brought from thence to Westminster; and the King in memory of her, caused in every place, where her body rested by the way, a stately cross of stone to be erected, with the Queen's image and arms upon it, as at Grantham; Woburn, Northampton, Stony-Stratford, Dunstable, St Albans,[377] Cheapside,[378] and Charing; from whence she was conveyed to Westminster, and there buried. This cross in Cheapside being like to these other which remain to this day, and being by length of time decayed, John Hatherley, Mayor of London anno 1441 procured license of King Henry 6th to re-edify the same in more beautiful manner, for the honour of the city; and had licence also to take up 200 fother of lead, for the building thereof, and other necessary places in the city.[379] This cross was then curiously wrought, at the charges of divers citizens. John Fisher, Mercer, gave 600 Marks towards it, the same was begin to be set up anno 1484 and was finished anno 1486 being the 2nd year of the reign of King Henry 7th Afterward it was richly gilt all over, anno

---

[376] Howell, p. 67.

[377] Commonplace author omits 'Waltham' from the list. Seems to be an oversight.

[378] Original refers to 'West Cheap'.

[379] Original explains that these are 'certain conduits and an old common granary'.

1522 against the coming of the Emperor Charles 5th into England. As also against the coronation of Queen Anne Bollen,[380] anno 1533. And it was new burnished against the coronation of King Edward 6th anno 1547 and it was again new gilt against the coming of Philip King of Spain[381] anno 1554.

Since which time, the said cross, having been[382] presented by divers juries (or quests of wardmote)[383] to stand in the highway to the let of carriages (as they alleged) but could not have it removed; that followed that in the year 1581 June the 20 in the night, the lowest image about the said cross (being of Christ's resurrection, of the Virgin Mary, King Edward the Confessor, and such like) were broken and defaced. Proclamation was made, that whosoever would discover the doers, should have 40 Crowns but nothing came to light; the image of the blessed Virgin, at that time was robbed of her Son, and her arms broken, by which she stayed him on her knees. Her whole body was also held with ropes, and lest likely to fall; but in the year 1595 was again fastened and repaired; and in the next year following, a new misshapen Son, as born out of time, all naked, was laid in her arms, the other images remaining broke as before. But on the East side of the same cross the steps being taken thence, under the image of Christ's resurrection defaced was set up a curious wrought tabernacle of gray marble, and in the same, an alabaster image of Diana, and water conveyed

---

[380] 'Bollen' added by commonplace author for clarification.

[381] 'Of Spain' added by commonplace author for clarification.

[382] 'bin' spelling appears in both Howell and commonplace book.

[383] Local court held in each of London's wards.

from the Thames, trilling from her naked breast, which continued for a time, but afterward, decayed. And in the year 1599 the timber of the cross at the top, being rotted within the lead, the arms thereof bending, were feared to fall, to the harm of some people; and therefore the whole body of the cross was scaffolded about; and the top of it taken down, intending in the place thereof to have set up a pyramid. But some of Queen Elizabeth's[384] honourable councillors directed their letters to Sir Nicholas Moseley the Mayor, by her Majesty's express command, concerning the cross, forthwith to be repaired, and placed again as it formerly stood. Not withstanding the cross stood headless above a year after, whereupon the said councillors, meaning not any longer to permit the continuance of such a contempt, wrote sharply to William Rider the then Mayor requiring him, by virtue of her Highness said former direction and command without any further delay, to accomplish her Majesty's most Princely care therein, respecting especially, the antiquity and continuance of the monument, and ancient ensign of Christianity, dated, Dec: 24 1560. After this a cross of timber was framed, set up, covered with lead, and gilded, the body of the cross downward, cleansed of dust, and the scaffolds carried thence. About 12 nights following, the image of our lady was again defaced by plucking off her crown, and her head too aloft; taking from her, her naked Child, and stabbing her in the breast. But in the year 1644, this ancient and visible a Monument or Ornament of the City of London, as all foreigners esteemed it, was during the

---

[384] 'her majesty's' in the original.

usurpation and tyranny of the Long Parliament[385] utterly demolished, and while the thing was a doing, there was a noise of many trumpets blew all the while. And thus much of the cross in Cheapside.[386]

57.[387] Kings, if present are in all places present and act, if absent they must rule per deputatem because by common indictment they cannot take notice of things done in their absence.[388] It hath therefore been the ancient course of the Kings of England to constitute Vice-gerents in their absence, giving them several titles, and several powers, according as the necessity of affairs required. Sometimes they were called Lord Warden or Lord Keeper of the Kingdom, and had there with the general power of a King[389] as it was with John Warren, Earl of Surrey, appointed thereto by King Edward the 1st who had not only power to command, but to grant, and the power extended both to England and Scotland and Peter Gaveston (though a foreigner) had the like power given him by Edward II over England.[390] Sometimes these

---

[385] Commonplace author has added his judgement of the Long Parliament and the idea that foreigners admired such crosses as the one at Cheapside.

[386] Final sentence also added by commonplace author to conclude that section.

[387] Bacon, p. 81 (1651).

[388] First sentence is added by commonplace author.

[389] Reference omitted: Rot. Pat. 24. E. 1. m.4.

[390] Reference omitted: Rot. Pat. 1. E. 2. m. 2. Commonplace author also omits sentence on the revenge taken on Gaveston by English nobles. Not interested? Or so familiar with this story that there was no need to write it down?

vice-gerents were called Lieutenants, which seemed to confer only the King's power in the Militia, as a Lieutenant General in an army. And thus Richard II made Edmund Duke of York, his Lieutenant of the Kingdom of England during his absence in Ireland, to oppose the entry of the Duke of Hartford into England afterwards called Henry IV and the other part of the royalty which concerned the revenues of the Crown, was entrusted to the Earl of Wiltshire, Sir John Bushy, Sir James Baggot, and Sir Henry Green. But more ordinarily, the King's power was delegated to one under both the titles of Lord Guardian of the Kingdom and Lieutenant within the same, such was the title of Henry Lacy, Earl of Lincoln, of Gilbert de Clare, Earl of Gloucester, and of Audomar de Valence,[391] Earl of Pembroke, all of them at several times so constituted by Edward II. So likewise did Edward III make his brother John of Eltham twice; Edward the Black Prince thrice, and Lionel Duke of Clarence and his brother Thomas each of them once, in several passages beyond the sea in the 3^d 5th 12th 14th 16th 19th 33th years of his reign[392] and Henry V gave likewise the same title and authority to the Duke of Bedford upon the King's voyage into France.[393] And afterward that Duke being sent over to second the King in his French wars, the Duke of Gloucester obtained the same place and power. But Henry VI added a further title of Protector and Defender of the Kingdom and Church of England that was first given to

---

[391] Reference omitted: Rot. Pat. 4 E. 2. Ps. 1. m. 18.

[392] Reference omitted: 'see the Paltent Rolls of those yeares.10 Hen. 5. p. 1 m. 9.'

[393] Reference omitted: 7 Hen. 5. m. 23

the Duke of Bedford, and afterward he being made Regent of France it was conferred on the Duke of Gloucester; and towards the latter time of Henry VI it was granted to Richard Duke of York.[394] This title of custos or Protector Regni Anglia, carried along with it a power, different from that of a King, only in honour and the person so adorned may be said to sway the Sceptre but not to wear the Crown.[395] And in truth if this title of the kingdom's guardianship be considered in its bare lineaments without lights and shadows, it will appear little better than a crown of feathers worn only for bravery, and nothing added to the real ability of the governing part of the kingdom. Neither were the persons of these magnificos so well deserving, nor did the kingdom expect any such matter from them. Edward I was a wise prince and yet in his absence chose his son, afterward Edward II to hold that place, he being then not above 14 years of age; and Edward II his wife, and the Lords of her party, were wise enough in their way, and yet they chose Prince Edward her son to be Custos Regni, then not 14 years old, his father in the mean time being neither absent from the Kingdom nor deposed,[396] but only dismissed from acting in the administration of the government. Edward III followed the same example for he first made his brother John of Eltham Custos Regni, and this he did 2 several times, once when he was but 11 year old, and afterward when he was about 14. Then he made his son, the Black

---

[394] Reference omitted: 32 H. 6. m. 7.

[395] Several paragraphs of the original missed out here discussing the minority of Henry VI.

[396] Reference omitted: Rot. Pat. 5. E. 3. p. 1. m. 16.

Prince upon several occasions 3 times Lord Warden of the Kingdom; once he being 9 year old, a second time when he was 11 and a third when he was about 14 years of age. Lastly the same King Edward appointed his son Lionel Duke of Clarence unto this place of Custos Regni when he was scarce 8 years old.[397] If therefore the work of a Custos Regni be such as may be well done by the infants of Kings as by the wise councillors or most valiant soldiers,[398] it is manifest, that this place is of little other use to the kingdom of England[399] than to serve as attire to a comely person to make it seem more fair because it is in fashion, nor doth it advance the value of a King one grain above what his personal endowments do deserve.

58.[400] The natural and original power of the King of England's Privy Council is very obscure because there hath been several degrees of them that occasionally have been used, all of whom may deserve the name of Privy Council in regard of the Parliament which is the most public council of all the rest, and always hath a general interest in all causes in the Kingdom.

The first of these is that which was called the Grand Council of the King, which as some conceive[401] was not the House

---

[397] Reference omitted: 'all which will appear upon the comparing their ages with the severall Rolls of 25 E 1. and 3, 5, 12, 14, 16, 19, E 3'.

[398] 'man' in original.

[399] 'commonwealth' in original

[400] Bacon, p. 28 (1651)/

[401] Original 'which I think'.

of Lords, who are called by summons, and were only to attend during the Parliament but a body made up of them, and other wise men of his own retinue, and of this it seems there was a constant body framed, that were sworn to that service;[402] for some in former times, as in those of King Edward III[403] were sworn both of the Grand Council, and the Privy Council, and so entered upon record.

The second of these councils was also a Great Council, and probably greater than the other; but this was called only upon some emergent occasion, and consisted of all sorts like a Parliament.[404] Of this there was an example in the Ordinances concerning of the Staple, which at first were made by the King's Prelates, Dukes, Earls, Lords and great men of the Kingdom one of every county and borough[405] called together for that end and even were called in the time of the same King Edward III. The results whereof were but as in point of trial for 6 months space and then were turned into a statute law in 27th and 28th of that King by several Parliaments then held. These 3 are Magna Concilia yet without power, further than as for advice because they had no other foundation, nor constant continuation.[406] Another Council remains more private than the other, and of more continual use, though not so legally founded, and this is called the King's Privy Council, not taking up a whole house, but only a chamber and a table, signifying rather

---

[402] Reference omitted: 16. E. 3. Memb. 5. in Dors.

[403] In original 'in these times', name of King added for clarification.

[404] In original 'yet was none'.

[405] Reference omitted: 27 E. 3. Stat. 2 28 E. 3. cap. 13.

[406] Bacon, pp. 28-29 (1651).

communication of advice than power of judicature, which more properly is in Banco[407] yet the power of this Council grew up virile and royal, and would acknowledge no peer but the Parliament as being the representation of it. The ambition thereof hath been great;[408] and the platform of the power of this Council[409] is in their oath.

1. That well and truly they shall counsel the King, according to their best care and power, [410] and keep well and lawfully his Councils.

2. That none of them shall accuse each other, of any thing which he had spoken in Council.

3. And that their lawful power, aid and counsel, they shall with their utmost diligence apply to the King's Rights.

4. And the Crown, to guard, and maintain, save, and to keep off from it, where they can without doing wrong.

5. And where they shall know of the things belonging to the Crown, or the Rights of the King, to be concealed, intruded upon, or subtracted, they shall reveal the same to the King.

---

[407] Meaning 'at the bench'.

[408] Sentence omitted from the original describing the desire of the Privy Council to keep power for themselves.

[409] Omits 'you may behold'.

[410] Reference omitted: Mag. Cart. Vet.

6. And they shall enlarge the Crown, so far as lawfully they may, and shall not council the King, in decreasing the rights of the Crown, so far as they lawfully may.

7. And they shall let no man (neither for love nor hate, nor for peace, nor strife) to do their utmost (as far as they can, or do understand) unto every man in every estate, right and reason, and in judgment and doing right, shall spare none, neither for riches nor poverty.

8. And shall take of no man without the King's leave, unless meat or drink in their journey.

9. And if they be bound by oath formerly taken, so as they cannot perform this without breaking that they shall inform the King and hereafter shall take no such oaths, without the King's consent first had.

All which in a shorter sum sounds in effect. First that they must be faithful councillors to the King's person, and also to his Crown, not to decrease the true rights, but to increase them, yet all must be done lawfully. And secondly, that they shall do right in judgment to take no fees nor any other oath in prejudice of this; the first of these concern the public, only at a distance; [411] the second concerns the King more immediately.

---

[411] Commonplace author omits a sentence about what would happen if the first rule is broken.

59.[412] The waters of the Bath in Somersetshire,[413] have an extraordinary actual heat and medicinal virtue in them which properties in them above other waters hath made divers curious to know the reason thereof; some impute it to wind, or air, or some exhalations shut up in the bowels of the earth, which either by their own nature, or by their violent motion and agitation, or attrition upon rocks, and narrow passages, do gather heat and so impart it to the waters. Others attribute this balneal heat unto the sun, whose all searching beams penetrating the pores of the earth do heat the waters. Others think this heat to proceed from quicklime which by common experience is found[414] to heat any water cast upon it, and also to kindle any combustible substance put upon it. And there are some that ascribe this heat to a subterranean fire, kindled in the bowels of the earth upon sulphury and bituminous matter; all these may indeed be general concurring causes but not the adequate, proper, and peculiar reason of balneal heats; and herein a late modern physician[415] hath got the start of any that ever writ of this subject, and goes to work like solid philosopher; for having treated of the generation of minerals, he finds that they have their seminaries in the womb of the earth, replenished with active spirits, which meeting with apt matter, and adjuvant causes, do proceed to the generation of several species according to the nature of the efficient, and fitness of the

---

[412] James Howell, *Epistolae Ho-elianae* (London, 1650), p. 165.

[413] Again, commonplace author removes first person narrative; original says 'I fell to contemplate...'

[414] 'we can find' in original.

[415] 'our learned countryman' in the original.

matter. In this work of generation as there is generatio vinus, so there is corruptio alterius[416], and this cannot be done without a superior power, which by moisture dilating itself, works upon the matter, like a leavening and ferment, to bring it to its own purpose. This motion 'twixt the agent spirit and patient matter, produces an actual heat, for motion is the fountain of heat, which serves as an instrument to advance the work; for as cold dulls so heat quickens all things. Now for the nature of this heat, it is not a destructive violent heat, as that of fire, but a generative gentle heat, joined with moisture nor needs it air by ventilation. This natural heat is daily observed by digging in the mines; so then whole minerals are thus engendering and in solutis principis,[417] by their liquid forms, and not consolidated into hard bodies (for then they have not [...] or virtue) they impart heat to the neighbouring waters; so then it may be concluded that the soil about [...] is a mineral vein of earth, and the fermenting gentle temper of the generative heat induction of the said minerals, do impart, and actually communicate this balneal virtue, and medicinal calefaction[418] to these waters.

60.[419] There are some who are thus professed opposites to that excellent ordinance of God, marriage; and who cannot

---

[416] Translation: 'creation of wine' and 'corruption of all others'.

[417] Translation: 'in the release of the principle'.

[418] 'medicinal heat' in the original.

[419] Although this topic is one that is common in early Protestant polemics as formerly celebate clergy justified their marriages, it does not appear to be a copy of a sermon that was printed in England in English. While its sentiments are similar to those of Luther, Calvin and Erasmus,

brook that it should (in opinion) be preferred before single life, in any man's judgment, or (in practice) be at all permitted to some men, namely to them that serve at the altar, for the papists teach that no man may think marriage equally excellent with virginity, nor any clergyman may meddle with it; but to abstain from it as from some foul sin. Which evident heresy and impiety of the papists, being by the Apostles' verdict 1 Tim: 4 1 3 a Doctrine of Devils. Hath none to abet it but his disciples. A gracious wife was a blessing to Adam in his innocence, even the confirmation of his present welfare, what man then, of son of man (except the man of sin, and son of perdition 2 Thes: 2.3) can with any colour of truth, account her an evil not to be touched and esteem any son of Adam, more holy, or more happy without her than they are to whom she is given. Were not all men ministers and clergymen (as well as others) in the loins of Adam when God spoke that word Gen 2. 18. It is not good for man to be alone, was it not spoke to Adam, and (in him) to all that were to come of him, even then when he (and all

---

it does not appear to have been a direct copy. Later Protestant polemics on marriage (such as Bacon and Milton) from the 17th century tend to focus on the nature of marriage and gender relations and even divorce rather than justifying it *vis a vis* celibacy. This paragraph mentions Bellarmine in the present tense: was the original written during his lifetime: 1542-1628? This leaves the possibility that it is the translation of a more obscure Protestant writer not published in English or has been copied from a manuscript or is a series of notes written from memory by the commonplace author having heard a sermon. It is unlikely to be notes in preparation for a sermon because there are no similar notes in this collection. A possibility is Goerg Calixtus's work on clerical celibacy published in Latin in Helmstadt in 1631 and Frankfurt in 1651. Calixtus mentions Bellarmine in his work against clerical celibacy. However, this would be an odd choice of source as every other book studied by the commonplace author is in English, published in London.

mankind) were without any such necessity of a wife as arises out of the least natural annoyance, or any other frailty whatsoever. And is that become no blessing to some men now, which was such happiness, when all men were at their best. Are those 2 universal and glorious ends which the Lord directly intended (in the institution of matrimony) to wit the world's multiplication, and the Church's propagation. And is the 3rd (which came in so accidentally by man's corruption) to wit, to become a remedy against unclean desires (which God in much mercy hath made marriage to be) a mere nullity to so many as (throughout the world) entertain the ministry: the more sinful and sacreligious is the false opinion and enforced practice of the papists, who by their popish denial of marriage (at once) stands guilty of a 3 fold theft, for it robs, heaven of saints; earth of men; and men of a powerful means to prevent sin. Ministers by their impurity of nature are as corrupt as others, and stand under the same necessities natural that all men do; shall they be made incapable of the remedy, who are as incident to the malady as any? Again the popish asserting of the single life or celibate hath been supported with infinite dishonour to God, with insufferable abuse, yea blasphemy of his Sacred word, and with unspeakable evils, and adulterous, incestuous, sodomitical villainies unnameable; in so much that there is no impure practice so hideously shameful or hellishly sinful, but hath been acted by this occasion; for these devoted Catholics, who being chaste in opinion, are so foul in conversation, that he who compares their opinions published in their treatises, with their practices detested in their histories, shall at once discover most hateful hypocrisy, and much horrible dishonesty. What single person can (with common sense) conceit his estate equal (or any thing near) so honourable as is the dignity of matrimony. Where did God ever honour celibacy, as he hath done matrimony? Can any man instance any honour in scripture appertaining to the former, which may carry any comparison with the latter. A crown of some fading flowers is sometimes set upon the head of virginity, but this is only the world's custom, not by God's prescription. The Romanists' reasons for a single life are silly and their arguments feeble, and Bellarmine their champion confesses he hath no scripture to avouch it, but to prove marriage a sacrament they lay about eagerly, yet the best members of their church (to wit their clergy) may not meddle with it; if a priest marry, he sins, and to prove it Pope Syricus who sat in the chair anno 385 most profanely wrested the pure word of God. Re: they that are in the flesh cannot please God, which was an impious exposition. Virginity is no sacrament, yet they hold that the priest that vows it doth merit. Matrimony is a sacrament and yet it is a mortal sin for any of that order to enter into it. If it is true single life is good but marriage in many respects is better. If once in the persecution of the church single life was accidentally preferred (not as any way more excellent, but as at that time, some way more expedient) may this conclude any perceived eminency it hath above marriages. And though it was said that once (considering the time) 1 Cor: 7.1 It is not good for a man to touch a woman, the church was then in distress, therefore during those days, it was best to be single, and it was spoken occasionally to some persons in the exigency of one time. Furthermore the voice of God Gen: 2.18 it is not good for man to be alone, again Eccles 4. 20 woe be to him that is alone, and this voice of God was of such force that the Apostle grants it lawful (even in the worst times) to take wives rather than to sin for want of them 1 Cor: 7.2 So then that is the general rule which was given to all persons; this is only a temporary exemption from it in some case; and which of the two must carry the truth, all men know. The members of the Church it's true are sometimes called virgins to teach them how pure and unspotted they should be, in all manner of conversation personally. But it is not virginity, but marriage that hath produced this threefold good, namely peopled the world, propagated the church and furnished heaven. To conclude, the opinion of the Romanists is so false, and their practices so foul in the particular of marriage; that if the wish of many good men that (if it be possible) the thoughts of their hearts may be changed not only herein, and in whatsoever strong delusions their minds are infatuated with and then prayers also to that God who hath thus far given them over, to judge themselves unworthy and incapable of the comfort of matrimony, may in due time draw them out of this, and all other darkness.

61.[420] In the famous province of Syria in Asia was that country which heretofore was called first the land of Chanaan of the son of Cham, the second son of Noah[421] who possessed it. It was also called the Land of Promise because God promised it to Abraham, and his son.[422] This country

---

[420] Gerard Mercator, *Historia Mundi* (London, 1635) page 427.

[421] 'second son of Noah' added by commonplace author.

[422] In original 'to our fathers Abraham, Isaac and Jacob'.

when the ancient inhabitants were beaten out, it was thirdly called Israel, of the Israelites who came in their places, so called from Jacob, Abraham's Grandchild, who was surnamed Israel and fourthly it was named Judea from the people of the tribe of Judah, Ptolomy [...] [...] ancient geographers do in the fifth place call it Palestina quas Philistin, or the land of the [...] of Philistines, a people of great note and a potent nation herein as the sacred scriptures do mention and sixthly, the holy land, because herein was wrought the work of man's redemption and salvation by Christ.[423]

This country is situated in the middle of the world between the 3^d and 4th Climates, the longest day being 14 hours and a quarter,[424] and between the Mediterranean, and Arabia; on which side beyond the River Jordan, it is encompassed with a continued ridge of mountains, and so it reaches from Egypt as some ancients[425] will have it, or as others from the Lake Sirbon, even to Phoenicia. The bounds thereof are these; it hath on the East Syria and Arabia, on the South the Desert of Paran, and Egypt; on the West the Mediterranean Sea; and on the North, the Mountain Lebanon. It is in length 200 miles, as some write,[426] but other hold that the length of it reaching on the North to the city of Dan, seated at the foot of the Mountain Lebanon (which was afterward called

---

[423] Reason for the naming is not given in the original.

[424] Original does not contain information about the climates and the longest day.

[425] Herodotus named in original.

[426] Nothing in original about the length of Israel. As previously the commonplace author is sourcing geographical information from elsewhere.

Caesarea Philippi) and so on the South to the city of Beersheba, is but 67 miles, every mile being an hour's journey, but the breadth which is to be taken from the Mediterranean Sea on the West, to Jordan on the East does contain in some places 16, in other places 18 of like miles. Yet hath the breadth been computed to be 50 miles of those miles by which the length is computed.[427] Of all countries it is chiefly commended for the wholesomeness of the air, fertility of the soil flowing with milk and honey, the winter being not too cold, nor the summer too hot:[428] that before the coming of the Israelites it maintained 30 Kings and afterward the 2 potent kingdoms of Israel and Judah in which David numbered 1300000 fighting men, besides them of the tribe of Benjamin and Levi.[429] These Israelites or Jews were a people of middle stature, strong of body, resolute and inconstant; but they are now accounted a perjorous vagabond nation, and great usurers.[430]

---

[427] This sentence does not appear in the original.

[428] Omits detail on the flora and fauna of Israel. Rejoins Mercator's text on page 428.

[429] Original does not mention number of David's soldiers or the tribes of Benjamin and Judah.

[430] Mercator's comments here are similarly anti-semitic, but with different emphasis. He described the mixed fortunes of the Jews and claimed that because they had been responsible for the crucifixion of Christ they suffered further: 'After that there ensued new calamities and miseries.' Manuscript concludes half-way down a page, with no indication that the author had finished his notes. Perhaps he intended to add more.

Bibliography of works consulted by commonplace author

Those in brackets are the possible alternative sources for the section copied from Purchas.

{*A Brief Relation concerning the discovery of New England* (London, 1622)}

Nathaniel Bacon, *A Historical and Political Discourse* (London, 1689)

Richard Baker, *A Chronicle of the Kings of England* (London, 1643)

Samuel Clarke, *A true and faithful account of the four chiefest plantations of the English in America to wit, of Virginia, New-England, Bermudus, Barbados*[...] (London, 1670)

G. H. *Memorabilia mundi, or, Choice memoirs of the history and description of the world by G.H* (London, 1670)

{Richard Hawkins, *The observations of Sir Richard Havvkins Knight, in his voiage into the South Sea. Anno Domini 1593* (London, 1622)}

Sir Thomas Herbert, *Some yeares travels into divers parts of Asia and Afrique. Describing especially the two famous empires, the Persian, and the great Mogull: weaved with the history of these later times as also, many rich and spatious kingdomes in the orientall India, and other parts of Asia; together with the adjacent iles. Severally relating the religion, language, qualities, customes, habit, descent, fashions, and other observations touching them. With a revivall of the first discoverer of America. Revised and enlarged by the author.* (London, 1638)

Peter Heylyn, *Cosmographie in four bookes : containing the chorographie and historie of the whole vvorld, and all the principall kingdomes, provinces, seas and isles thereof* (London, 1652)

James Howell, *Epistolae Ho-Elianae* (London, 1645-50)

James Howell *Londinopolis* (London, 1657)

King James, *The Gunpowder Treason* (London, 1679)

{Sylvester Jordain, *A Discovery of the Barmudas* (London, 1610)}

{Marc Lescarbot, *Nova Francia* (London, 1609)}

Gerardus Mercator, *Historia Mundi*, (London, 1635)

Samuel Purchas, *Purchas his pilgrimes In fiue bookes*[...](London, 1625).

Nicolas Sanson, *Cosmography and Geography in two parts* (London, 1682)

Johannes Sleidanus (or John Sleidan), *The General History of the Reformation from the errors of the Church of Rome* (1689)

{John Speed, *A prospect of the most famous parts of the vvorld*[..]. (London, 1631)}

John Stow, *Survey of London* (London, 1598)

{Richard Whitbourne, *A Discourse of the New Found Land* (London, 1620)}

Catherine Armstrong

Dr. Catherine Armstrong received her Ph.D. in History from the University of Warwick. She is a Lecturer in Modern American History at the University of Loughborough and was previously based at Manchester Metropolitan University.